Gendering the Middle East

Gender, Culture, and Politics in the Middle East
Leila Ahmed, Miriam Cooke, and Simona Sharoni
Series Editors

Gendering the Middle East

Emerging Perspectives

Edited by

Deniz Kandiyoti

Syracuse University Press

First Edition 1996

96   97   98   99   00   01   6   5   4   3   2   1

Published in the United States by Syracuse University Press,
Syracuse, New York 13244–5160,
by arrangement with I.B.Tauris & Co. Ltd
London WC1A 2HY

ISBN 0-8156-2695-9 (cl) — ISBN 0-8156-0339-8 (pb)

CIP data available from the publisher upon request.

Manufactured in the United Kingdom

Contents

Contributors

Joanna de Groot works in the history department and the Centre for Women's Studies at the University of York. Her interests are shaped by research and writing on Iran in the nineteenth and twentieth centuries, by work on the gendered historical dynamics of imperial, ethnic and racial encounters, and by the scholarly and practical involvement in women's contribution to social and political action. She is currently working on texts about political cultures in Iran c.1870–1980, and on gender, sexuality and empire in British and French history.

Deniz Kandiyoti is senior lecturer in the Department of Anthropology and Sociology of the School of Oriental and African Studies, University of London. She is editor of *Women, Islam and the State* (Macmillan and Temple University Press, 1991) and has written extensively on issues of gender.

Sheila Hannah Katz is an independent scholar. She has taught at Harvard and Tufts Universities and writes on issues of gender, conflict and the Middle East. She has recently completed a dissertation at Harvard University on 'Women and Gender in Jewish and Palestinian Nationalisms before 1950: founding and confounding the boundaries'.

Annelies Moors, an anthropologist at the University of Amsterdam and Leiden University, is the author of *Women, Property and Islam: Palestinian experiences 1920–1990*, (Cambridge University Press, 1995) and co-editor of *Discourse and Palestine* (Amsterdam: Het Spinhuis, 1995). She has published on biographical method, on women and Islamic law, and on women and Orientalism. She is presently researching photographs of women in Palestine.

Parvin Paidar completed her doctorate at Birkbeck College, University of London. She has research interests in the fields of Middle Eastern women's studies, refugee studies, human rights and development. She is author of *Women in the Political Process of Twentieth-century Iran* (Cambridge: Cambridge University Press, 1995). She has previously published under the pen name of Nahid Yeganeh.

Hoda El Sadda is Assistant Professor of English at Cairo University. She is co-editor of Hagar, a series of books on women's issues published in Arabic by Dar Sina. She has translated two collections of Arabic short stories into English: *Evening Lake* by Ibrahim Aslan (General Book Organization, 1990) and *Such a Beautiful Voice* by Salwa Bakr (General Book Organization, 1990). She is currently working on autobiographical writing by Egyptian women.

Rosemary Sayigh teaches at Beirut University College. She is author of *Palestinians: from peasants to revolutionaries* (Zed Press, 1979) and *Too Many Enemies: the Palestinian experience in Lebanon* (Zed Press, 1994). Over the past decade she has researched the situation of Palestinian refugees in Lebanon, focusing particularly on women and has published many articles on the subject.

Simona Sharoni, an Israeli feminist and peace activist, is Assistant Professor of Peace and Conflict Resolution Studies at the American University of Washington, DC. She is author of *Gender and the Israeli–Palestinian Conflict: The politics of women's resistance* (Syracuse University Press, 1995) and is currently working on a book on the dynamics of identity and conflict.

Preface

This volume had modest beginnings since it arose neither from the design of an editor seeking to achieve some grand thematic unity, nor from a self-conscious intention to systematically take stock of recent developments in gender studies in the Middle East. It originated in the desire of some members of the Middle East Study Group in England to evaluate the extent to which gender as an analytic category had been incorporated into studies on the Middle East and to assess the theoretical and political implications of such an analytic move. The original intention of assembling these deliberations in a special issue of the *Review of Middle East Studies* was modified and extended by soliciting further contributions. During the entire process, the editor was forcibly struck by the fact that numerous scholars had, in fact, incorporated gender-aware perspectives and methodologies into their work in a wide variety of thematic and disciplinary contexts. However, the inroads that such scholarship might have made were neither explicitly reflected upon nor adequately evaluated. Furthermore, the otherwise diverse work of these scholars had some features in common. While part of their concern may have been to engage with and interrogate the canons of their respective disciplines, they were also uniformly committed to gender analysis as a tool for social criticism. They also felt challenged by the difficult task of articulating feminist perspectives and modes of analytic intervention.

This discovery inspired the title of this book, which is explicitly exploratory. It makes no claims to cover the region in geographic terms, nor to represent theoretical debates within it exhaustively. Rather, it explores the extent to which gender analysis has succeeded in not only informing but in challenging established views of culture, society, politics and literary production in the Middle East. It is probably no coincidence that five out of the eight chapters of the volume (those by Katz, Moors, Paidar, Sayigh and Sharoni) are based on recently completed doctoral dissertations, with many more doubtless to follow. What these contributions suggest, is that we have already traversed some of the considerable distance separating an initial preoccupation with 'women's condition' in the Middle East to developing gendered perspectives on diverse aspects of culture and society. Although the articles do not amount to any kind of programmatic statement, they jointly point the way to a 'deepening' of gender studies across the social sciences and the humanities in the Middle East. They also both illustrate and contribute to new directions in feminist scholarship.

Deniz Kandiyoti (Chapter 1) provides an overview of contemporary developments in feminist scholarship and evaluates the manner and extent of their incorporation into Middle East studies. She argues that feminist scholarship in the West and studies on women in the Middle East have been following parallel and partially overlapping trajectories and that Middle East studies have been characterized by a selective incorporation of the broader agendas generated by feminist criticism. This selectivity is best explained with reference to the historical and local specificities of the development of feminist currents and women's studies in the region. Both the discursive limitations of existing scholarship and the potential for new directions are explored.

Joanna de Groot (Chapter 2) attempts to capture these new directions specifically in relation to Iranian studies. She detects three moments in the development of gender studies; recuperation, redefinition and transformation, which she sees reflected in studies on contemporary Iran. The initial emphasis on making women visible and the preoccupation with the role of Islam, stimulated by the 1979 Islamic revolution, are increasingly making way for a new scholarship on Iran which defines gender as a constitutive element of society.

Parvin Paidar (Chapter 3) argues that gender discourse has been at the heart of Iranian politics since the turn of the century. She traces the changing articulations between Islam and feminism and documents the development of Islamist feminisms since the advent of the Islamic Republic in 1979. Her thoughtful conclusions concerning the possibility of coalitions between different feminist tendencies in post-revolutionary Iran echo Nicholson's prescriptions for a post-modern feminist agenda 'that we think about feminist politics as the coming together of those who want to work around the needs of women where such a concept is not understood as necessarily singular in meaning or commonly agreed upon'.[1]

Annelies Moors (Chapter 4) provides a sophisticated

demonstration of how a focus on gender modifies our understanding of the assumed connections between property and power
in the Middle East. Using her anthropological fieldwork in
Palestine, she cogently argues that women's relations to property
are mediated by a complex network of gender relations which are
derivable neither from legal codes nor from the nature of the
property itself. She illustrates her contention with reference to
women's diverse 'inheritance strategies' which highlight the features of the local gender system as well as the changes produced
by migration and the increasing reliance on wage incomes. Finally,
she is able to bring her material to bear on a relationship that was
incompletely understood and theorized by historians and anthropologists.

Sheila Katz's (Chapter 5) historical incursions into Palestinian
and Jewish texts prior to 1950, reveal the deeply gendered nature
of nationalistic discourse, and its intimate connection to constructions of masculinity and femininity. She argues that nationalist
narratives construct new masculinities, feminize and eroticize 'the
land', mould and co-opt women in the service of modernization
and that, finally, women both contest and collude with these constructions and imaginings. She also shows how these changing
images of men, women and community contributed to shaping
specific power relations between and among Jews and Arabs.

Simona Sharoni (Chapter 6) ventures into one of the last
bastions of social science to resist the incursions of feminist
revision, namely international relations.[2] She subjects the Israeli–
Palestinian accord to scrutiny through a gendered lens which
reveals the marginalization of women as political actors, the
submergence of their peace movements and the masculinist and
militaristic underpinnings of the accord which inevitably lead to
a flawed and limited understanding of conflict resolution and
peace. She proposes a number of feminist approaches aimed at
destabilizing status quo conceptions of what constitutes the 'centre'
and 'margins' of political life and at questioning the practices of
social exclusion upon which our notions of community are based.

Hoda El Sadda (Chapter 7) helps us comprehend the various
phases traversed by women's writing in Egypt, a trajectory symptomatic of gender hierarchies in both society and the literary establishment. She does so through a sensitive treatment of Salwa Bakr
and an appreciation of her path-breaking work. Using Showalter's
stages of women's writing—the feminine, the feminist and the

female—El Sadda periodizes Egyptian women writers' contributions and situates them historically. She notes the particular resistance encountered by women writers who are invited to partake in a presumed 'universal' perspective which corresponds to that of the male literary establishment. She finally shows how Salwa Bakr, through both the choice of her themes and her innovative use of language, transcends the dualities of male/female, public/private, classic/colloquial and finds a voice of her own.

Rosemary Sayigh (Chapter 8) provides us with a lucid account of her fieldwork in a Palestinian camp in Lebanon in a manner that interweaves three histories: that of the Shateela camp in the 1980s, her own history as a researcher, and that of the research project which evolved and changed with the circumstances. She writes candidly about the difficulties of squaring her own interest in gender as a feminist anthropologist with the research community's agenda of national resistance and struggle. She illustrates critical dilemmas about positionality, accountability and ethics in doing feminist research and how these informed her choice of research techniques and priorities.

Taken in their totality, these articles represent forms of scholarly intervention that share important commonalities despite their disciplinary diversity; they foreground gender as a means of understanding, decoding and ultimately challenging aspects of the social and cultural phenomena under investigation. This should constitute a solid common denominator for a feminist agenda.

Notes

1. Linda Nicholson, 'Interpreting gender', *Signs*, vol. 20, no.1, 1994, p. 102.

2. In their introduction to a recent volume Rebecca Grant and Kathleen Newland explain both the sources of this resistance and the imperative for change. Rebecca Grant and Kathleen Newland (eds), *Gender and International Relations* (Milton Keynes: Open University Press, 1991).

Contemporary Feminist Scholarship and Middle East Studies

Deniz Kandiyoti

Acknowledging the global nature of the production and circulation of ideas has acquired the status of a truism, yet there are surprisingly few attempts to systematically analyse points of intersection, dialogue and confrontation between discourses emanating from distinct socio-historical locations, especially when these are situated outside the West.[1] Feminist scholarship does not escape this charge despite its avowed commitment to transcending boundaries—both in a geographical and analytical sense. More often than not we remain locked in our respective parochialisms as we utilize vocabularies that may appear superficially similar, yet often have different associations, meanings, resonances and political consequences in the different contexts in which we live and work. A painstaking process of critical reflection on the nature and historicity of the contexts within which knowledge is produced, although clearly necessary, has barely begun with respect to feminist scholarship in the Middle East. This chapter is primarily devoted to furthering such an endeavour.

In what follows, I will be examining the manner and extent to which advances in feminist scholarship have been reflected in studies in and about the Middle East, and whether these in turn have modified our ways of seeing and thinking. I will be arguing that feminist scholarship in the West and studies on women in the Middle East have been following parallel and partially overlapping trajectories and that Middle East studies have been characterized by a selective incorporation of the broader agendas generated by feminist criticism, alongside home-grown debates firmly grounded in local historical and political specificities. I am not assuming that feminist discourse in the Middle East necessarily emerges as a response to, or in dialogue or confrontation with Western currents of thought, but rather acknowledging the effects which various forms of institutionalization of women's studies in the academy, in international organizations and transnational networks may produce. I will first attempt to outline the main thrust of contemporary feminist scholarship and evaluate studies in and about the Middle East in relation to both these theoretical developments and other international and local agendas. I will conclude with an evaluation of prospects for the future.

Developments in Feminist Scholarship

The development of feminist scholarship since the 1960s, corresponding to the second wave of feminist activism in the West, has been uneven both across social science disciplines and in different geographical locations. It is therefore unrealistic to attempt a comprehensive account of the field beyond a necessarily schematic and selective presentation. Keeping these limitations in mind, I propose a periodization covering three main phases which are not strictly chronological, but rather represent different 'moments' of feminist theorizing.

The First Phase: Combating Androcentric Bias

This phase was characterized by efforts to establish the field of 'women's studies' and provided an extensive documentation and critique of androcentric bias in the social sciences. Feminist scholars produced accounts of how the absence of women as social actors and the fact that social theory and history were written from a male perspective constituted major weaknesses in the very explanatory frameworks of their disciplines.

In history, the first phase consisted in setting the record straight by giving voice to the perspectives and experiences of women.[2] The 'women's history movement' of the 1970s produced landmark works such as Sheila Rowbotham's *Hidden from History* and Renata Bridenthal and Claudia Koontz's *Becoming Visible*.[3]

Anthropologists were likewise engaged in a critique of the categories and assumptions of their discipline.[4] Michelle Rosaldo and Louise Lamphere's *Woman, Culture and Society* and Reyna Rapp Reiter's *Towards an Anthropology of Women* marked a turning point in feminist anthropology.[5] Anthropologists revived the debate on the origins of the seemingly universal subordination of women. While some concluded that gender asymmetry was universal others, revisiting Engel's thesis, argued that the relatively egalitarian relations prevailing among native populations with a communal economy were transformed by colonialism and the cash nexus. Although the debate on origins was divisive and fairly inconclusive, it stimulated new interpretations of anthropological data.

Psychologists were primarily concerned about the fact that most generalizations in their discipline were based on data and observations drawn from male subjects and that the human norm was, in fact, a male norm. For example, Carol Gilligan's *In a Different Voice* critiqued Kohlberg's theory of stages of moral development which took male patterns as the norm and suggested that men and women exhibit different types of moral orientation.[6] By and large, psychology in general and psychoanalysis in particular were denounced as part of the ideological apparatus that sanctions conventional gender roles in the name of adjustment and mental health. Psychoanalysis was, however, recovered by some feminists both in its Freudian/Lacanian version (as in the case of Juliet Mitchell and some post-structuralists) and in its object relations variety (as with Nancy Chodorow).[7] Major divisions nevertheless remained both between different strands of psychoanalysis and between psychologically informed feminisms in general and their post-structuralist critics, pointing to their ultimate essentialism.[8]

In economics, the categories of labour and value came under close scrutiny, especially the fact that women's unpaid labour was unaccounted for and hence rendered invisible. Among Marxists, the so-called 'domestic labour debate' raised important questions concerning the place and function of women's unpaid labour in relation to capital, especially with respect to their role in the reproduction of the labour force. In a pioneering study of world patterns, *Women's Role in Economic Development*, Ester Boserup documented the extent to which women's labour in fact contributes to Third World economies and the uneven effects of modernization on men and women.[9] The 'women in development' studies that blossomed during the 1970s were to have a considerable impact on work in the Middle East, as we shall see later. In a broader context, this approach stimulated the documentation of 'gender gaps' through the numerous studies on women in Third World development initiated during International Women's Year in 1975 and the UN Decades that followed it.

Feminist revision also took place in sociology[10] and political science[11] and by the 1980s led to a critique of epistemology which asserted that the very way science constructs knowledge is gendered.[12] This led to a search for feminist methodologies and alternative ways of defining subject-object relationships in social research.[13]

This phase provided the initial challenge to mainstream social science and produced a rich harvest of studies making women visible as historical, social, economic and political actors. It also matured and evolved from an attempt to include 'women's perspectives' to subjecting the central analytic categories of disciplines to critical scrutiny.

The Second Phase: Accounting for the Subordination of Women

Although there are no clear lines of demarcation between this and the preceding phase, it could be argued that attempts to account for gender asymmetries increasingly crystallized around distinct orientations in feminist theory and practice reflecting liberal, Marxist/socialist, psychoanalytic and, more recently, post-structuralist influences.

Liberal feminists located the causes of women's subordination in the customary and legal constraints blocking women's access to the public domain and in prejudices (sexism) and stereotypes concerning their capabilities. This approach generated valuable empirical studies on the domestic and work lives of women and different facets of discrimination and sex-typing. However, it was criticized for failing to appreciate the systemic and deep-rooted nature of gender subordination and for not providing a framework to explain it.

In the search for such a framework, significant divergences developed between radical and socialist feminists. Radical feminists invoked the notion of patriarchy as a timeless, universal system of male domination perpetuating the oppression of women as a group through the control of their sexuality and procreative capacity. Their research agendas reflected their theoretical premises with special attention to issues such as motherhood, compulsory heterosexuality, rape, pornography and domestic violence.[14] The main criticism raised against this notion of patriarchy was that it tended towards a biological essentialism that provided little basis for an understanding of historical and cultural variations.[15] Feminists working within a Marxist framework attempted to resolve this problem by linking patriarchy to different modes of production. However, the specific nature of exploitation based on gender was submerged and subordinated to class exploitation in many such accounts. Socialist feminists offered a further corrective by theorizing capitalism and patriarchy as two separate but interdependent systems of exploitation. There followed a period of intense debate concerning the nature of the relationships between capitalism and patriarchy.[16] By the mid-1980s this debate was showing signs of increasing sterility despite some important contributions.[17]

However, empirical research on the relations between the changing international division of labour and sexual divisions of labour grew apace as scholars and activists with an interest in Third World development started making use of the major insights gained from Western feminist theory whilst attending to issues of immediate local relevance.[18] Issues pertaining to gender and class increasingly appeared on a global, more international research agenda in conjunction with inequalities and maldistribution on a world scale.[19] Many also called into question the universalist pretensions of existing feminist theories emanating from mainly white, middle-class scholars by highlighting the specificity of Third World women's experiences.[20]

Meanwhile, feminist appropriations of post-structuralism were leading to a questioning of the notion of the unity of women as a self-evident category and their 'oppression' as a unitary phenomenon. Reflecting a broad mix of influences (some mutually contradictory) ranging from Derrida's deconstructionism, Foucault's discourse theory, Lacanian psychoanalysis and Lyotard's post-modernism, post-structuralists argued that the major objective of a feminist project should be to analyse the construction of the category 'woman' through the practices that produce sexual difference and analyse how subordination is reproduced through a multiplicity of practices, discourses and institutions.[21] Indeed, Barrett and Phillips suggest that a gulf separates the feminist theory of the 1970s and the 1990s and that the earlier consensus has been destabilized by the onslaughts of post-structuralist critics on categories such as oppression, patriarchy and sexual difference itself.[22] At the point when all universal narratives about emancipation and the category of 'woman' were being called into question, feminism itself as a viable a political project could appear problematic, a question that has exercised many attempting to theorize the links between feminism and post-modernism.[23] The debate is by no means conclusive, with some expressing suspicion about the fact that the concept of subjecthood is decreed problematic at the very historical juncture when marginalized peoples (women, blacks, the colonized) are beginning to find their voice,[24] and others embracing post-structuralism as a source for productive feminist agendas.[25] However, the incremental and longer term effect of these debates has been to produce a gradual but significant shift from 'woman' to 'gender' as a central analytic category.

The Third Phase: From Woman to Gender

By the mid-1980s the purview of the field had substantially shifted from women's studies to the study of gender, namely analyses of the ways in which all aspects of human society, culture and relationships are gendered. Nicholson reminds us that within feminism the term 'gender' is used in two distinct and, indeed, contradictory ways. On the one hand, it is used to depict that which is socially constructed, in contrast to 'sex' which is assumed to be biologically given. On the other hand, gender refers 'to any social construction having to do with the male/female distinction, including those constructions that separate "female" bodies from "male" bodies.'[26] According to this definition, sex is subsumable under gender and not separate from it since our constructions of the body are themselves subject to social interpretation and redefinition. Gender has therefore been transformed into an increasingly inclusive category denoting an expression of difference within a field of power relations. Or, as succinctly put by Joan Scott, 'Gender is a constitutive element of social relationships based on perceived differences between the sexes, and gender is a primary way of signifying relationships of power.'[27] Lorber also defines gender as an all-pervasive social institution that 'establishes patterns of expectations for individuals, orders the processes of everyday life, is built into the major social organizations of society, such as the economy, ideology, the family and politics, and is also an entity in and of itself'.[28]

This shift in emphasis was greeted with a certain amount of scepticism by some as the wholesale abandonment of a central tenet of feminism, namely that women constitute a unified category around whose concerns an emancipatory project could be articulated. In particular, the fact that the field was redefined to include the study of men and masculinities (both in relation to the subordination of women and to other types of institutionalized forms of power and domination)[29] generated some controversy. The 'new men's studies' received a mixed reception from scholars

who felt that this field appears to be constructing itself as an adjunct
to feminism, appropriating its major insights, but giving it only
partial credit and competing for scarce institutional resources.[30]
More generally, de Groot and Maynard caution us against a
depoliticizing tendency whereby 'the rhetoric of gender is increasingly being used in a benign and neutral fashion without addressing
questions of power, privilege and women's subordination.'[31]

Outside Western academe, however, and in the Middle East in
particular, where the infrastructure for women's studies teaching
and research is only beginning to develop, there are clearly far
fewer stakes around these demarcations, hence more latitude in
judging the analytic advantages implicit in different approaches.
In this respect, I would agree with Joan Acker that the focus on
gender has opened up new perspectives on institutions such as the
state, science, the military and formal organizations, arenas from
which women are typically excluded, and which are seldom analysed in a manner cognizant of gender.[32] Clearly, such perspectives
can be put to powerful uses and broaden the reach of feminist
social criticism. The work of R.W. Connell, for instance, provides
us with important insights on the intersections between gender
and other social institutions, including the state.[33] Cynthia
Cockburn's work on technological change highlights the complex
dynamics involved in the reproduction of masculinity and privilege,
illustrating the linkages between the two.[34] The question which
remains to be answered is the extent to which this analytical move
has stimulated further integration of gender perspectives into the
social sciences, a serious concern which cannot be dealt with in
this chapter.

In what follows, I will set scholarship on the Middle East against
this brief general excursus into women's and gender studies in
order to evaluate its specificities, strengths, limitations and possible
future directions. I will argue that feminisms in the Middle East
have been both intensely local, grappling with their own histories
and specificities, and international, in that they have been in
dialogue, both collaborative and adversarial, with broader currents
of feminist thought and activism.

Scholarship on Women in the Middle East

Feminist scholarship and advocacy in the Middle East has followed
a distinctive trajectory reflecting both its engagement with local

debates and its dialogue with broader currents of thought, from the turn of this century to the present. Attempting to provide an account of this trajectory is impossible without doing violence to the 'local dialects' which feminism has developed within specific locations and in response to specific historical events.[35] Indeed, one of the most salient features of scholarship in the region is that it has evolved against a background of highly politicized and emotionally charged reflection on key political events and turning points which exert a potent, if sometimes subterranean, influence. The most obvious are specific histories of decolonization, although more contemporary events also shape the discursive field. Nelson, for instance, identifies the 1967 defeat of the Arabs in the Six Day War against Israel as one such moment prompting critical self-reflection among Arab intellectuals.[36] The continuing struggle of the Palestinians for national self-determination has likewise exerted a profound, and sometimes divisive, influence on scholars of the region. The advent of the Islamic Republic in Iran provided yet another turning point, and an arena for renewed debate and self-reflection, not only among Iranian scholars but a much broader constituency of scholars and feminists. More local and less visible struggles have also informed the concerns and writings of feminists in the region and sometimes only finely attuned ears, trained in the 'local dialects', can detect the sub-texts, omissions, silences, overt and coded protests. Despite these serious qualifications, I propose a crude periodization of the main currents of feminist thought and scholarship in the Middle East in order to identify some of its formative moments.[37]

The First Wave: Feminism and Nationalism

The first wave of feminist writing in the Middle East is associated with movements for social reform and modernization during the era of post-colonial state formation spanning the periods between the nineteenth and early decades of the twentieth centuries. This period exhibits striking discursive parallels between Turkey, Iran and Egypt, establishing a lasting framework for discussions of the 'woman question'. In all these cases, nationalism was the leading idiom through which issues pertaining to women's position in society were articulated.[38] I have argued elsewhere that there have been persistent tensions between the modernist trends in nationalism, which favoured an expansion of women's citizenship rights

women cultural carriers

national & women

and social equality, and the organicist, anti-modernist, strands which were concerned about the dilution and contamination of cultural values and identity in a post-colonial context.[39] Women's stake in nationalism has been both complex and contradictory. On the one hand, nationalist movements invite women to participate more fully in collective life by interpellating them as 'national' actors: mothers, educators, workers and even fighters. On the other hand, they reaffirm the boundaries of culturally acceptable feminine conduct and exert pressure on women to articulate their gender interests within the terms set by nationalist discourse. In that sense, feminisms are never autonomous but bound to the signifying networks of the contexts which produce them.

In the Middle East the combination of predominantly Muslim societies' encounters with an imperialistic West, the flawed nature of agendas for national development and the preoccupation with Islam as a marker of cultural identity, have constrained the discursive possibilities of feminist scholarship and established styles of debate exhibiting remarkable resilience through time. This is evident in the fact that the debate on the compatibility of Islam with women's emancipation, harking back to Qasim Amin,[40] is still on the agenda in the 1980s and 1990s.

The strong identification of cultural authenticity with Islam has meant that feminist discourse could only legitimately proceed in two directions: either denying that Islamic practices are necessarily oppressive or asserting that oppressive practices are not necessarily Islamic.

The first strategy, in its polemical variant, counterposes the dignity of the protected Muslim woman against the commodified or sexually exploited Western woman.[41] Academic enquiries into the various concrete contexts in which Muslim women live may be found in the work of anthropologists whose materials reveal that women lead rich, rewarding and meaningful lives behind the apparent limitations set by segregation and that they wield considerable influence and power.[42] It must be acknowledged here that such work constituted a welcome and essential departure from stereotypical, Orientalist depictions of subjugated women entrapped in the fast-frozen relations of an atemporal Islam.[43] However, as incisively noted by Abu-Lughod, this 'battle against shadow stereotypes' has, in time, developed into a rhetorical ploy, which made the documentation of women's 'real' lives an end in itself, encouraging a certain parochialism *vis-à-vis* feminist anthropology,[44] and, indeed, *vis-à-vis* feminist scholarship more generally.

The second strategy, in its polemical variant, depends on a 'golden age' myth of an uncorrupted original Islam against which current discriminatory practices may be denounced as falling short of truly Islamic ideals. In its academic variant, this strategy produces work which challenges uniformly patriarchal interpretations of Islam by presenting more radical alternatives as part and parcel of Islamic tradition. This, in turn, opens up the possibility of articulating 'indigenous feminisms' which do not owe their origin or inspiration to Western sources of influence. Scholars have favoured this strategy in the 1980s, at a time when the cultural hegemony of Islamist tendencies was on the ascent, mandating a feminist intervention. Sophisticated examples of this genre may be found in Fatima Mernissi's *Women and Islam: An historical and theological enquiry* [45] and Leila Ahmed's *Women and Gender in Islam.*[46] Although the implications of the first strategy could be potentially conservative and the second clearly more radical, they occupy a similar discursive space.

It is significant, however, that the debates about women and Islam which were initiated during the first wave of feminist writing were muted and submerged for a considerable period only to re-emerge with renewed vigour in the 1980s. In the intervening period, questions pertaining to women's status were incorporated into broader accounts of social change and development emanating from the major social science paradigms.

The Second Wave: The Rise of Social Science Paradigms and Developmentalism

The 1950s and 1960s witnessed the emergence and consolidation of social science disciplines in the Middle East and the incorporation of questions about the family and women's roles into broader discourses about social transformation, namely modernization theory and Marxism. Modernization theory presupposed a movement from tradition to modernity affecting all facets of social life.[47] Disparities in gender relations within the family and society at large could henceforth be explained in terms of relative degrees of modernization.[48] The rural, uneducated, overly fertile and male-dominated came to represent the traditional with the urban, educated, child-centered and companionate representing the modern.

Since this model, especially in its Parsonian variant, homogenized a wide variety of non-Western societies under the rubric of 'traditional', culturally specific forms of women's subordination were neglected in favour of broad indicators of socio-economic development such urbanization, education and industrialization.

This discourse about transition had its counterpart in Marxist theory which counterposed the feudal and semi-feudal to the capitalist/industrial, again rendering gender relations epiphenomenal and derivable from the properties of broader socio-economic structures. In retrospect, it may seem natural enough that during a period of state-led economic growth and political consolidation in the post-war period, there was a sense of both urgency and confidence about possibilities for national development in most countries of the Middle East which reflected itself in scholarship. Various forms of social inequity, including those based on gender, could be treated as social ills that should be overcome once societies had attained the requisite level of development.

It is in the period leading up to the 1975 UN International Women's Year, which promoted a thoroughgoing critique of modernization theory, that a second wave of feminist writing was stimulated in the Middle East, as in many other parts of the world. The women in development (WID) literature contested the notion that the benefits of modernization had trickled down to women and even argued that women were, in places, disempowered by losing access to some of their traditional avenues of livelihood and social participation. The concept of disadvantage based on gender was firmly back on the agenda, but remained tightly enmeshed in concerns about development. This had limitations, but it also had its uses, especially for those anxious to break out of Orientalist discourses on the Middle East. The fact that Middle Eastern women also led material lives which could be amenable to analysis through the general concepts of social science opened up the possibility of their integration into the theoretical mainstream. Important work such as Judith Tucker's *Women in Nineteenth-century Egypt* [49] demonstrated the potential of historically informed materialist analyses. In the more strictly development-related literature the inclusion of Middle Eastern women under the broader rubric of 'Third World' women, a category justifiably found wanting by critics such as Chandra Mohanty, [50] served to loosen the grip of Orientalist exclusivity, which sealed off Muslim women into a world of total non-commensurability. This opened the way for more comparative perspectives and materially grounded analyses of women in the Middle East.[51]

The Third Wave: Dialogues within Feminism

It is also after the 1970s that we witness more significant inroads being made by Western academic feminism into Middle Eastern scholarship. This influence was mediated through different constituencies with somewhat differing agendas: Western scholars working on the Middle East with a high stake in bringing their Middle Eastern material in line with the various paradigms of academic feminism, Western-trained Middle Eastern scholars, expatriate or locally resident, with multiple reference groups in Western academe and their countries of origin, and locally trained scholars, some with access only to works in translation and to more localized debates.

The result was a selective and uneven incorporation of the various concepts of feminist theory into Middle East studies and the emergence of distinctive, local styles of polemic and scholarship. To take but one example, Michelle Rosaldo's invocation of the public/private dichotomy as the basis for the subordination of women[52] seemed to find a natural home in a region where this dichotomy appeared to take concrete forms in patterns of spatial segregation and female confinement. Thus, although Rosaldo developed these concepts within a much broader frame of reference, it is in Middle East studies that we find their most detailed elaborations.[53]

There followed a rich output of writing and research on women in the Middle East which has, in time, become increasingly differentiated along disciplinary and thematic lines.[54] Some of this writing displays what might superficially appear as a paradox; the simultaneous depiction of Middle Eastern women as weak and oppressed or as the epitome of strength and solidarity. Inevitably, the familism and corporate orientation of many Middle Eastern societies was being experienced as stifling and limiting by some, and as rewarding and more meaningful than their own Western backgrounds by others, and such experiences were, sometimes unreflexively, finding their way into scholarship.[55] The preoccupation with Western 'ethnocentrism' also emerged as an enduring concern, with scholars experiencing varying degrees of need to position themselves vis-à-vis the subjects of their study as the 'benevolent' or 'sympathetic' Other.[56]

There were also a significant number of Western-trained scholars in the Middle East who, although familiar with academic feminism in the United States and Europe, had to operate both with more limited resources and in environments more actively inimical to their concerns. Their multiple reference groups could become a source of both inspiration and alienation. The fact that they were differently positioned *vis-à-vis* the subjects of their study made them accountable in quite different ways. Most importantly, the relevance of their scholarship to the immediate concerns and day-to-day struggles of women in their societies was not something they could easily overlook.[57]

Finally, there were also scholars writing exclusively in local languages and not necessarily interested in engaging with Western academe. Some never left the tradition of first wave feminist writing and kept alive a polemic on women's rights, national identity and Islam which resurfaced in academic writing in the 1980s.[58] This created a complex and heterogeneous landscape which cross-cut but did not correspond to the concerns of Western feminist scholarship and activism.

Furthermore, the various currents of Western feminism were unevenly represented in the Middle East. The liberal feminist approach, with its emphasis on removing 'obstacles' to gender equality through changes in legislation, improving access to education and paid employment and combating sexist attitudes was immediately intelligible and relatively easy to adapt to local conditions. It is far from having exhausted its considerable radical potential, especially in contexts where women's rights have been subjected to curtailment and redefinition. This approach is implicit in most sociological studies inspired by modernization theory in the 1950s and 1960s and later in the 'women in development' studies with their emphasis on closing 'gender gaps' in education, access to resources and legal status.

Socialist feminisms also found a home in the various applications of the world systems and dependency theories to the Middle East. If one wing of the 'women in development' literature reflected a liberal world-view, another strand emanated from neo-Marxist theories of development and underdevelopment. This work reflected an engagement with the systemic effects of under-development and their impact on women in a manner that sometimes privileged colonialism and neo-colonialism as the prime movers of gender inequality. Hatem suggests, with considerable

justification, that this represents an extension of nationalist discourse, since Middle Eastern patriarchies can hardly be understood solely with reference 'to those aspects of their political
economies and societies that serve colonial or post-colonial
interests'.[59] Nonetheless, the terms of production and reproduction,
class and patriarchy found their way into many accounts of the
condition of women.[60]

Here again, local agendas have added original twists to the
usage of certain terms. The concept of patriarchy is a case in
point.[61] Hisham Sharabi introduced the concept of 'neo-patriarchy'
to designate post-colonial state formations in the Middle East in
a manner which modifies and inflects the designations commonly
associated with it in Western feminist theory. He develops the
term to characterize both the macro-structures of the economy
and polity and the micro-structures of the community and family.[62]
Although it may be a questionable category from the vantage
point of political economy or political theory, it nonetheless
emerges as a provocative item of cultural criticism and an attempt
to formulate a language to talk about forms of authoritarianism
at all levels of society. Feminism, in this context, emerges as a
radical challenge to the very premisses upon which such authoritarianism is based, an idea also strongly present in the work of
Fatima Mernissi.[63] Sharabi posits a natural affinity between feminism and non-Western critical discourse,[64] while Mernissi highlights
the subversive potential of universalistic discourses about human
rights and citizenship in societies where submission to the will of
God and temporal rulers constitute powerful alternative paradigms. Both see feminism as an inseparable component of the
democratic impulse in their societies.

It is noteworthy that neither radical feminism nor psychoanalysis were to have any significant impact on mainstream studies
about women in the Middle East. Indeed, with the exception of
the early works of Nawal El Saadawi[65] which confronted women's
oppression as sexual beings and raised questions about violence,
abuse, incest, rape and clitoridectomy and Fatima Mernissi's earlier
work on Islamic constructions of female sexuality,[66] there was little
emphasis on sexuality as such.[67] This could be explained with
reference to both a resistance against delving into culturally taboo
areas and a reaction against the gender essentialism implicit in
some radical feminist theorizing which bears some resemblance
(albeit with different implications) to the categories deployed by

Islamic fundamentalism.[68] If, according to some feminists, women's essentially different natures qualify them to be the custodians of a more environmentally friendly, less violent and more democratic world, these natures may be invoked with equal force to disqualify them from everything except domestic and child-rearing roles. I would venture to suggest that the category of 'Western feminism', often deployed as a pejorative term in the Middle East to denote the general irrelevance of a diversionary, alien project, is constructed through a conflation of all feminist tendencies with some of its radical feminist variants. Indeed, a perceived emphasis upon the primacy of individual autonomy and gratification, including sexual liberation, and the denunciation of men as the main enemy could easily go against the cultural grain in societies where both men and women are tightly enmeshed in familistic networks of mutual rights and obligations, where both sexes may be labouring under much harsher forms of economic and political oppression and where different possibilities exist for cross-gender coalitions.

The Fourth Phase: Where to from Here?

The current phase of feminist theorizing, briefly presented in the first part of this chapter, poses new challenges the implications of which are as yet hard to detect. Despite internal divergences within feminist currents prior to the 1980s they did display some important commonalities. They assumed that women constituted a category sharing a common oppression, that the reasons for their oppression were amenable to causal explanation (despite sharp disagreements on the causes themselves) and that meaningful forms of struggle and association could be evolved to achieve their liberation.

The late 1980s have witnessed a breakdown of this consensus and set the scene for what might be characterized as an internal crisis about 'difference' which originated in the West. In the United States white, middle-class feminism came under attack for displaying racist and ethnocentric tendencies. In Europe, this internal critique coincided with non-European migrants' and ethnic minorities' demands for their rights to cultural distinctiveness and was punctuated by events such as the Salman Rushdie affair in England and the *foulard* debate in France.[69] The policies of multiculturalism and identity politics in the West thus exerted a significant influence on feminist theorizing. The combined effects of post-structuralism and debates about multi-culturalism are also being reflected in scholarship on the Middle East.

Questions about difference and the analysis of power hierarchies implicit in constructions of the 'Other' have, of course, been central to critiques of Orientalism initiated by the inspiring work of Edward Said. Post-Orientalist scholarship had a great deal to say about gender since representations of the 'Oriental' woman were integral to depictions of harem life, exoticism and the erotic.[70] This stimulated a new genre whereby textual analysis and the study of representations gained significant momentum across all social science disciplines, extending well beyond comparative literature and literary criticism where they originated. Julie Marcus writing on Turkey, for instance, castigates the producers of Orientalist texts quite extensively and, although she is an anthropologist, relies mainly on secondary sources confining her own ethnographic data principally to one chapter.[71] There have been other texts written from a Foucauldian (or Saidian) perspective, some more illuminating than others, mainly emanating from Western rather than local sources.

This scholarly strategy, especially in disciplines normally mandating actual fieldwork, might have been a partial response to the occasionally crippling effects of having to seek authority for one's authorial voice with reference to one's positionality, who one *is*, rather than the analytic rigour or credibility of the arguments being elaborated. Indeed, deconstructing texts emanating from one's own culture—preferably from male authors with imperial connections—is a much safer enterprise than having to engage with the far messier realities of contemporary social life and the perplexing cross-currents evident in the politics of gender in contemporary Middle Eastern societies. But the more serious disservice which some varieties of post-Orientalist scholarship may unwittingly perform resides in the fact they often remain locked into the categories of colonizer vs colonized, East vs West, Islam vs Christendom, Western Self vs Native Other in ways that keep our gaze fixed upon the discursive hegemony of the West. This usually occurs to the detriment of more self-referential analyses of culture and society which should inform local feminist criticism. Ironically, it is principally in the writings of Islamists that such constructions are mirrored and utilized as justifications for counter-hegemonic moves, where the universalism of the Enlightenment, denounced as an imperial project, may be pitted against an Islamic universalism based on principles of an immutable divine order. It is these very categories that we need to reject in order to recognize the complexity and heterogeneity of Middle Eastern societies and open up new spaces for social criticism.[72]

The multi-culturalism debate in the West was based on a recognition of the internal heterogeneity of modern societies and an attempt to accommodate difference within democratic pluralistic polities.[73] Identifying an 'external' site for the production of difference in Middle Eastern societies, namely the West and its internal allies, in contradistinction to the 'truly indigenous', conveniently by-passes the need to take on board the equally heterogeneous, ethnically and religiously diverse and ideologically divided nature of such societies and potentially delegitimizes the voices of those politically defined as marginal. In short, the transposition of concerns about 'difference' to the Middle East has often taken polemical forms which have not necessarily favoured the development of productive feminist agendas but instead, to paraphrase Lazreg, have turned difference into 'mere particularity', potentially letting Orientalism in through the back door.[74]

Yet, there are other possibilities implicit in current developments and in the shift from women to gender, alluded to earlier, which have not yet been fully exploited. The abandonment of grand narratives to account for the subordination of women is making room for detailed analyses of the different institutional realms through which gender hierarchies are reproduced and has broadened the research agenda to include a much wider variety of cultural practices. In this perspective, social institutions do not merely reflect some unitary patriarchal logic but are the site of power relations and political processes through which gender hierarchies are both created and contested. Families, educational institutions, the law, the market, the state and the military, all contribute to and are shaped by cultural constructions of gender, often producing complex and mutually contradictory effects. These institutions and practices have received surprisingly little detailed attention in relation to the production of gender in the Middle East. Tucker, for instance, draws our attention to the fact that even the family, whose centrality is axiomatic in Middle Eastern studies, has hardly been the object of any detailed research that reveals the variability of household formations in the Arab world through time and space.[75] The same argument could easily be made in relation to other social institutions, most particularly those which appear to exclude women. A gender-aware focus on social institutions has the additional advantage of necessarily including a temporal dimension and a sensitivity to changes in the global contexts which shape and constrain local agendas. Although this may further fragment the vocabularies and terms of reference of feminist scholarship, it may nonetheless constitute a productive development if it ensures the diffusion of gender-aware perspectives throughout the humanities and social sciences in the Middle East.

Conclusion

The central argument of this chapter is that advances in feminist scholarship have been incorporated into studies about the Middle East in a partial and selective manner. The historical connection between feminism and nationalism in the Middle East has left an enduring legacy of concerns around the effects of cultural imperialism which has discouraged a systematic exploration of the local institutions and cultural processes, centrally implicated in the production of gender hierarchies and in forms of subordination based on gender. Social science paradigms, namely modernization theory and Marxism (with its dependency theory variants) have unwittingly reinforced this tendency by focusing on macro-processes of social transformation at a level of generality which rendered an engagement with local cultural specificities irrelevant. This was mirrored by grand narratives within feminist scholarship itself which attempted to pinpoint universal causes for the subordination of women. The abandonment of such narratives has produced contradictory effects. On the one hand, there is an emphasis on 'difference' which may potentially degenerate into unprincipled forms of relativism or, on the contrary, lead to more refined conceptions of political alliance and coalition-building. On the other hand, more context-dependent and micro-level explanatory frameworks may yield new ingredients for an 'internal' critique which has, by and large, tended to elude feminist scholarship in the Middle East. It would be fair to conclude that such scholarship now stands at a cross-roads; it will take a great deal of courage, imagination and commitment to realize its full potential.

Notes

1. It is possible to argue that this is precisely the task that post-colonial scholarship, which analyses the mutually constitutive relationship between Western imperialist discourse and colonized subalternity, has set itself. See for instance: Patrick Williams and Laura Chrisman (eds), *Colonial Discourse and Post-Colonial Theory* (London: Harvester Wheatsheaf, 1993). However, I find the term 'post-colonial' limiting and limited for an understanding of the contemporary circulation of feminist ideas in the academy, in international organizations and in various types of transnational networks.

2. Joan Wallach Scott, 'Women's history and the rewriting of history' in C. Farnham (ed.), *The Impact of Feminist Research in the Academy* (Bloomington: Indiana University Press, 1987). The difference between reinstating women as historical actors and making gender a central category of historical analysis is masterfully rendered in Joan Wallach Scott, *Gender and the Politics of History* (New York: Columbia University Press, 1988).

3. Sheila Rowbotham, *Hidden from History* (London: Pluto Press, 1973); Renata Bridenthal and Claudia Koontz, *Becoming Visible* (Boston, Mass.: Houghton Mifflin, 1977).

4. Louise Lamphere, 'Feminism and anthropology' in Farnham (ed.), *The Impact of Feminist Research.*

5. Michelle Rosaldo and Louise Lamphere, *Woman, Culture and Society* (Stanford: Stanford University Press, 1974); Rayna Reiter (ed.), *Toward an Anthropology of Women* (New York: Monthly Review Press, 1974).

6. Carol Gilligan, *In a Different Voice* (Cambridge, Mass.: Harvard University Press, 1982).

7. Juliet Mitchell, *Psychoanalysis and Feminism* (Harmondsworth: Penguin, 1975); Juliet Mitchell and Jacqueline Rose (eds), *Feminine Sexuality: Jacques Lacan and the École Freudienne* (London: Macmillan, 1982); Nancy Chodorow, *The Reproduction of Mothering* (Berkeley: University of California Press, 1978).

8. For a critique of both Gilligan and Chodorow see Nancy Fraser and Linda Nicholson, 'Social criticism without philosophy: an encounter between feminism and postmodernism', *Theory, Culture and Society*, vol. 5, nos 2–3, 1988: 373–94.

9. Ester Boserup, *Women's Role in Economic Development* (London: Allen and Unwin, 1970).

10. Ruth Wallace (ed.), *Feminism and Social Theory* (Newbury Park, California: Sage, 1989); Dorothy E. Smith, *The Everday World as Problematic: A feminist sociology* (Toronto: University of Toronto Press, 1987); Judith Stacey and Barrie Thorne, 'The missing feminist revolution in sociology', *Social Problems*, vol. 32, 1985: 301–16; Rosemary Compton and Michael Mann (eds), *Gender and Stratification* (Cambridge: Polity Press, 1986).

11. Susan Okin, *Women in Western Political Thought* (London: Virago, 1980); Jean Elshtain, *Public Man, Private Woman* (Oxford: Martin Robertson,

1981); Carol Pateman, *The Sexual Contract* (Cambridge: Polity Press, 1988); Jane Evans et al. (eds), *Feminism and Political Theory* (London: Sage, 1986); Seyla Benhabib and Drucilla Cornell (eds), *Feminism as Critique: Essays in the politics of gender in late capitalism* (Oxford: Basil Blackwell, 1987).

12. Sandra Harding and Merrill B. Hintikka (eds), *Discovering Reality: Feminist perspectives on epistemology, metaphysics, methodology and philosophy of science* (Dordrecht: D. Reidel, 1983); Sandra Harding, *The Science Question in Feminism* (Ithaca N.Y.: Cornell University Press, 1986); Donna Haraway, 'Situated knowledges: the science question in feminism and the privilege of partial perspective', *Feminist Studies*, vol. 4, no. 3, 1988: 575–99; Smith, *The Everyday World*; Evelyn Fox Keller, *Reflections on Gender and Science* (New Haven: Yale University Press, 1985).

13. Joan Acker, Kate Barry and Joeke Esseveld, 'Objectivity and truth: problems in doing feminist research', *Women's Studies International Forum*, vol. 6, no. 4, 1983: 423–35; Shulamith Reinharz, 'Experiential analysis: a contribution to feminist research' in G. Bowles and D. Klein (eds), *Theories of Women's Studies* (London: Routledge and Kegan Paul, 1983); Judith Stacey, 'Can there be a feminist ethnography?', *Women's Studies International Forum*, vol. 11, no. 1, 1988: 21–7; Beth Hess and Myra Marx Ferree (eds), *Analyzing gender: A handbook of social science research* (Newbury Park, CA.: Sage Publications, 1987); Lila Abu-Lughod, 'Can there be a feminist ethnography?', *Women and Performance: A journal of feminist theory*, vol. 5, no. 1, 1990: 7–27.

14. For example Shulamith Firestone, *The Dialectic of Sex* (New York: Bantam Books, 1979); Adrienne Rich, *Of Women Born* (New York: W.W. Horton, 1979); Adrienne Rich, 'Compulsory heterosexuality and lesbian existence', *Signs*, vol. 5, no. 4, 1980: 631–60; Susan Brownmiller, *Against Our Will* (New York: Simon & Schuster, 1975); Susan Griffin, *Pornography and Silence* (New York: Harper & Row, 1981).

15. Hester Eisenstein, *Contemporary Feminist Thought* (London: Allen & Unwin, 1984); Lynne Segal, *Is the Future Female? Troubled thoughts on contemporary feminism* (London: Virago Press, 1987); Caroline Ramazanoglu, *Feminism and the Contradictions of Oppression* (London: Routledge, 1989).

16. As in Mitchell, *Psychoanalysis*; Heidi Hartmann, 'The unhappy marriage of Marxism and Feminism: towards a more progressive union' in Lydia Sargent (ed.), *Women and Revolution* (London: Pluto Press, 1981) and other essays in the same volume; Zillah Eisenstein, *The Radical Future of Liberal Feminism* (New York: Longman, 1981). Mitchell argued that while economic relations are ordered by capitalism, patriarchy is the ideological form of women's oppression internalized in the unconscious. She thus reinstated psychoanalytic theory as providing an adequate account of how the law of patriarchy actually works. In contrast, Hartmann viewed patriarchy as a structure of social relations with a material base in men's control over women's labour power. Eisenstein, on the other hand, saw

patriarchy and capitalism as fused into a single system of capitalist-patriarchy. For a useful overview also see Michele Barrett, *Women's oppression today: The Marxist/feminist encounter* (London: Verso, 1988, revised edition).

17. An issue of the British journal, *Sociology* (vol. 23, no. 2, 1989), seems particularly indicative of the state of the debates at the end of the 1980s. This issue features two analytically sophisticated attempts by Malcolm Waters ('Patriarchy and viriarchy: an exploration and reconstruction of concepts of masculine domination, pp. 193–211) and Sylvia Walby ('Theorising patriarchy', pp. 213–34) to theorize patriarchy as a multi-dimensional phenomenon, thereby avoiding the reductionisms implicit in earlier formulations. A rejoinder by Joan Acker ('The problem with patri-archy', pp. 235–40) contends that a focus on patriarchy as a system or structure that is analytically independent of others ultimately leaves intact the patriarchal assumptions buried in theories about the other systems and leaves mainstream social science unmodified. For·a fuller statement of a comprehensive theory of patriarchy see Sylvia Walby, *Theorising Patriarchy* (Oxford: Basil Blackwell, 1990).

18. June Nash and Maria-Patricia Fernandez Kelly (eds), *Women, Men and the International Division of Labor* (Albany, N.Y.: SUNY Press, 1985); Irene Tinker (ed.), *Persistent Inequalities: Women and world development* (New York: Oxford University Press, 1990); Kate Young, Carol Wolkowitz and Rosslyn McCullagh (eds), *Of Marriage and the Market: Women's subordination in inter-national perspective* (London: CSE Books, 1981); Kathryn Ward (ed.), *Women Workers and Global Restructuring* (Ithaca, N.Y.: ILR Press, 1990); Bina Agarwal (ed.), *Structures of Patriarchy: State, community and household in modernising Asia* (London: Zed Books, 1988).

19. Gita Sen and Caren Grown, *Development, Crises and Alternative Visions: Third World women's perspectives* (New York: Monthly Review Press, 1987); Lourdes Beneria and Martha Roldan, *The Crossroads of Class and Gender: Industrial homework; subcontracting and household dynamics in Mexico City* (Chicago and London: The University of Chicago Press, 1987); Maria Mies, *Patriarchy and Accumulation on a World Scale* (London: Zed Press, 1986).

20. Chandra Mohanty, 'Under Western eyes: feminist scholarship and colonial discourses', *Feminist Review*, 30, Autumn 1988: 61–88; Floya Anthias and Nira Yuval-Davis,'Contextualizing feminism—gender, ethnic and class divisions' in Terry Lovell (ed.), *British Feminist Thought* (Oxford: Basil Blackwell, 1990); bell hooks, *Feminist Theory: From margin to center* (Boston: South End Press, 1984); Elizabeth Spelman, *Inessential Woman: Problems of exclusion in feminist thought* (Boston: Beacon, 1988); Cherrie Moraga and Gloria Anzaldua (eds), *This Bridge Called My Back: Writings by radical women of color* (Watertown, Mass.: Persephone, 1981).

21. For an overview see C. Weedon, *Feminist Practice and Post-structuralist Theory* (Oxford: Basil Blackwell, 1987). Some cultural feminists who challenge the notion of gender as dual, oppositional and fixed are: Judith

Butler, *Gender Trouble: Feminism and the subversion of identity* (London: Routledge, 1990); Donna Haraway, *Simians, Cyborgs and Women: The reinvention of nature* (New York and London: Routledge, 1991); Jane Flax, *Thinking Fragments: Psychoanalysis, feminism and postmodernism in the contemporary West* (Berkeley: University of California Press, 1990); Parveen Adams and Elizabeth Cowie (eds), *The Woman in Question* (London: Verso, 1990).

22. Michele Barrett and Anne Phillips (eds), *Destabilizing Theory* (Cambridge: Polity Press, 1992).

23. Linda Alcoff, 'Cultural feminism versus post-structuralism: the identity crisis in feminist theory', *Signs*, vol. 13, 1988: 405–36; Linda Nicholson (ed.), *Feminism/Postmodernism* (New York: Routledge, 1990); Flax, *Thinking Fragments*.

24. Nancy Harstock, 'Rethinking modernism: minority vs majority Theories', *Cultural Critique*, vol. 7, 1987: 187–206.

25. See Judith Butler and Joan W. Scott (eds), *Feminists Theorize the Political* (New York and London: Routledge, 1992).

26. Linda Nicholson, 'Interpreting Gender', *Signs*, vol. 20, no. 1, 1994: 79–105.

27. Scott, *Gender and the Politics of History*, p.42.

28. Judith Lorber, *Paradoxes of Gender* (New Haven and London: Yale University Press, 1994), p. 1.

29. As examples of the numerous recent volumes and edited collections see J. Hearn and David Morgan (eds), *Men Masculinities and Social Theory* (London: Unwin Hyman, 1990); Harry Brod (ed.), *The Making of Masculinities: The new men's studies* (Boston: Allen & Unwin, 1987); Michael S. Kimmel, *Changing Men* (Newbury Park: Sage, 1987); Victor J. Seidler, *Rediscovering Masculinity* (London: Routledge, 1989); Lynne Segal, *Slow Motion: Changing masculinities, changing men* (London: Virago, 1990); Andrea Cornwall and Nancy Lindisfarne (eds), *Dislocating Masculinity: Comparative ethnographies* (London: Routledge, 1994).

30. See for example, Judith E. Canaan and Christine Griffin, 'The New Men's studies: part of the problem or part of the solution?' in Hearn and Morgan, *Men, Masculinities*.

31. Joanna de Groot and Mary Maynard, 'Facing the 1990s: Problems and possibilities for Women's Studies' in de Groot and Maynard (eds), *Women's Studies in the 1990s: Doing things differently?* (London: Macmillan, 1993), p. 154.

32. Acker: 'The problem with patriarchy'; also Joan Acker, 'Hierarchies, jobs and bodies: a theory of gendered organizations', *Gender & Society*, vol. 4, 1990: 139–58.

33. Robert W. Connell, *Gender and Power: Society, the person and sexual politics* (Stanford: Stanford University Press, 1987); Robert W. Connell, 'The state, gender and sexual politics: theory and appraisal', *Theory and Society*, vol. 19, 1990: 507–44.

34. Cynthia Cockburn, *Brothers: Male dominance and technological change* (London: Pluto Press, 1983); *Machinery of Dominance: Women, men and technical know-how* (London: Pluto Press, 1985).

35. I hasten to add that these 'local dialects' exist within so-called Western feminism itself despite the more fluid and rapid circulation of ideas. Thus, different European feminisms (French, British and German) have their own genealogies and undergo interesting transformations once they cross the Atlantic. Australian writing also exhibits strong specificities despite the fact that it shares in an Anglo-Saxon linguistic universe.

36. Cynthia Nelson, 'Old wine, new bottles: reflections and projections concerning research on women in Middle Eastern studies' in Earl L. Sullivan and Jacqueline S. Ismael (eds), *The Contemporary Study of the Arab World* (Alberta: Alberta University Press, 1991).

37. The most serious limitation of this overview is that a rich literature based on Arabic, Turkish and Persian language sources is not adequately covered, although some key texts exist in translation.

38. See for instance Parvin Paidar, *Women and the Political Process in Twentieth-century Iran* (Cambridge: Cambridge University Press, 1995), Beth Baron, *The Women's Awakening in Egypt: Culture, society and the press* (New Haven and London: Yale University Press, 1994), Deniz Kandiyoti, 'End of empire: Islam, nationalism and women in Turkey' in Deniz Kandiyoti (ed.), *Women, Islam and the State* (London: Macmillan, 1991).

39. Deniz Kandiyoti, 'Identity and its discontents: women and the nation', *Millenium*, vol. 20, no. 3, 1991: 429–43.

40. Qasim Amin, the Egyptian reformer, is the author of *Tahrir al-Mar'a* (The liberation of woman) published in 1899 who advocated education for women, the reform of the laws on polygamy and divorce and, most controversially, the abolition of the veil. He followed other Muslim modernists such as Abduh and al-Tahtawi.

41. Laura Nader, 'Orientalism, occidentalism and the control of women', *Cultural Dynamics*, vol. 2, no. 3, 1989: 324–55.

42. For an extensive and thoughtful review of such work see Nelson, 'Old wine, new bottles'. Separate mention must be made of the important work of Elizabeth W. Fernea whose popular ethnograhies *Guests of the Sheikh: An ethnography of an Iraqi village* (New York: Anchor Books, 1965), edited works E.W. Fernea and B. Bezirgan (eds), *Middle Eastern Muslim Women Speak* (Austin: University of Texas Press, 1977); E.W. Fernea (ed.), *Women and the Family in the Middle East: New voices of change* (Austin: University of Texas Press, 1985) and numerous ethnographic films familiarized large Western audiences with the region.

43. Pathbreaking criticism of such depictions may be found in Edward Said's, *Orientalism* (Harmondsworth: Penguin, 1985), although he has relatively little to say about gender specifically. Critiques of Western representations of Middle Eastern women may be found in Malek Alloula, *The*

Colonial Harem (Minnesota: Minnesota University Press, 1986); Rana Kabbani, *Europe's Myths of Orient* (London: Macmillan, 1986); Judy Mabro (ed.), *Veiled Half-Truths: Western travellers' perceptions of Middle Eastern women* (London: Tauris, 1991).

44. Lila Abu-Lughod, 'Zones of theory in the anthropology of the Arab world', *Annual Review of Anthropology*, vol. 18, 1989: 267–306.

45. Fatima Mernissi, *Women and Islam: An historical and theological enquiry* (Oxford: Basil Blackwell, 1991).

46. Leila Ahmed, *Women and Gender in Islam* (New Haven and London: Yale University Press, 1992).

47. For a classic statement of this position see Daniel Lerner, *The Passing of Traditional Society: Modernizing the Middle East* (Glencoe, Illinois: Free Press, 1958).

48. See for example Safia Mohsen, 'The Egyptian woman: between modernity and tradition' in Carolyn Matthiason (ed.) *Many Sisters: Women in cross-cultural perspective* (New York: Free Press, 1974).

49. Judith Tucker, *Women in Nineteenth-century Egypt* (Cambridge: Cambridge University Press, 1978).

50. Mohanty, 'Under Western eyes'.

51. An early example of such work may be found in Nadia Youssef, *Women and Work in Developing Societies* (Population Monograph Series, Berkeley: University of California at Berkeley, 1974). Also see Mona Hammam, 'Women and industrial work: the case of Chubra el Kheima', *Arab Studies Quarterly*, vol. 11, 1980: 50–9; Judith Gran, 'The impact of the world market on Egyptian women', *Merip Reports*, 58, 1977: 3–7; Cynthia Myntti, 'Yemeni workers abroad: the impact on women', *Merip Reports*, 15, no. 4, 1984; Mona Hammam, 'Labor migration and the sexual division of labour', *Merip Reports*, 95, 1981: 3–5; Deniz Kandiyoti, 'Sex roles and social change: a comparative appraisal of Turkey's women' in Wellesley Editorial Committee (ed.), *Women and National Development* (Chicago and London: Chicago University Press 1977); Deniz Kandiyoti, 'Women and household production in Turkey' in K. and P. Glavanis (eds), *The Rural Middle East* (London: Zed Books, 1990).

52. Michelle Zimbalist Rosaldo, 'Woman, culture and society: a theoretical overview' in Rosaldo and Lamphere, *Woman, Culture & Society*.

53. As a classic example see Cynthia Nelson, 'Public and private politics: women in the Middle Eastern world', *American Ethnologist*, vol. 1, no. 3, 1974: 551–63.

54. One only has to compare pioneering volumes such as Lois Beck and Nikki Keddie (eds), *Women in the Muslim World* (Cambridge, Mass. and London: Harvard University Press, 1978) with the later volume by Beth Baron and Nikki Keddie (eds), *Women in Middle Eastern History: Shifting boundaries in sex and gender* (New Haven and London: Yale University Press, 1991) to verify this statement. The first volume was multi-disciplinary,

featuring contributions from anthropologists, historians, sociologists and political scientists who were only united by their common interest in the region. The second volume is based overwhelmingly on the contributions of historians pointing to a growing specialist constituency of scholars working on gender within the field of Middle Eastern history.

55. These are aspects of Middle Eastern life which must inevitably colour researchers' experiences yet have received surprisingly little theoretical elaboration. A notable exception may be found in the work of Suad Joseph, 'Gender and relationality among Arab families in Lebanon', *Feminist Studies,* vol. 19, no. 3, 1993: 465–86; 'Connectivity and patriarchy among urban working-class Arab families in Lebanon', *Ethos,* vol. 21, no. 4, 1993: 452–84.

56. Interestingly, a more self-reflexive stance on researchers' positionality appeared at the point when indigenous scholars started reflecting on their fieldwork experiences. See Soraya al-Torki and Camillia El Solh (eds), *Studying Your Own Society: Arab women in the field* (New York: Syracuse University Press, 1988).

57. Nelson suggests that 'as more Middle Eastern scholars turn their gaze inward upon their own societies and ultimately upon themselves' new paradigms will emerge and research will increasingly become 'indigenized'. In fact, the two ethnographies she mentions in this connection, namely Lila Abu-Lughod's *Veiled Sentiments: Honor, modesty and poetry in a Bedouin society* (Berkeley: University of California Press 1986) and Soraya Al-Torki's *Women in Saudi Arabia: Ideology and behavior among the elite* (New York: Columbia University Press, 1986) were carried out by anthropologists who were fully attuned to the canons of their discipline and to developments within it as well as to the communities they were studying.

58. Analyses of 'home-grown' genres of writing on women in Arabic, Persian and Turkish could contribute a great deal to our understanding of the genealogies of the 'local dialects' in feminism I referred to earlier. This would, however, constitute a separate project, since beyond the translation of certain key texts, no attempts have yet been made to undertake such analyses in a comparative framework.

59. Mervat Hatem, 'Toward the development of Post-Islamist and Post-nationalist feminist discourses in the Middle East' in Judith Tucker (ed.), *Arab Women: Old boundaries, new frontiers* (Bloomington: Indiana University Press, 1993).

60. See Mervat Hatem, 'Class and patriarchy as competing paradigms for the study of Middle Eastern women', *Comparative Studies in Society and History,* vol. 29, no. 4, 1987: 811–18. A more recent attempt to elaborate an analytic framework situating the Middle East within the world capitalist system and analysing women's status in relation to the sex/gender system, class and the state may be found in Valentine M. Moghadam, *Modernizing Women: Gender and social change in the Middle East* (Boulder and London: Lynne Rienner, 1993).

61. For a critique of the conflation of Islam and patriarchy see Deniz Kandiyoti, 'Islam and patriarchy: a comparative perspective' in Baron and Keddie, *Women in Middle Eastern History*.

62. Hisham Sharabi, *Neopatriarchy: A theory of distorted change in Arab society* (Oxford: Oxford University Press, 1988).

63. Fatima Mernissi, 'Democracy as moral disintegration: the contradiction between religious belief and citizenship as a manifestation of the ahistoricity of Arab identity' in Nahid Toubia (ed.), *Women and the Arab World* (London: Zed Books, 1988); *Islam and Democracy: Fear of the modern world* (London: Virago, 1993).

64. Hisham Sharabi (ed.), *Theory, Politics and the Arab World: Critical responses* (London: Routledge, 1990).

65. Nawal El Saadawi, *The Hidden Face of Eve: Women in the Arab World* (London: Zed Press, 1980).

66. Fatima Mernissi, *Beyond the Veil: Male-female dynamics in a modern Muslim society* (New York and London: Schenkman Publishing Company, 1975) and Fatna Sabbah, *Women in the Muslim Unconscious* (New York and Oxford: Pergamon Press, 1984).

67. This absence was noted in Nikki Keddie, 'Problems in the study of Middle Eastern women', *International Journal of Middle East Studies* vol. 10, 1979: 225–40.

68. See for instance Barbara F. Stowasser, 'Religious ideology, women and the family: the Islamic paradigm' in B.F. Stowasser (ed.), *The Islamic Impulse* (London and Sydney: Croom Helm, 1987).

69. In France, the right of Muslim girls to wear headscarves (*foulards*) in school became a hotly debated topic, dividing the secularists who want to avoid insignia of religious particularisms and those defending the 'cultural' rights of Muslims.

70. For a critique see Nancy Tapper, 'Mysteries of the harem: an anthropological perspective on recent studies of women of the Muslim Middle East', *Women's Studies International Quarterly*, vol. 2, 1979: 481–7; Leila Ahmed, 'Western ethnocentrism and perceptions of the harem', *Feminist Studies*, vol. 8, 1982: 521–34; Irvin C. Schick, 'Representing Middle Eastern women: feminism and colonial discourse', *Feminist Studies*, vol. 16, no. 2, 1990.

71. Julie Marcus, *A World of Difference: Islam and gender hierarchy in Turkey* (London: Zed Books, 1992). However, Marcus's invocation of 'purity law' in Islam as the basis of all social organization and gender hierarchy in Turkey makes one wonder how far, in fact, the argument against orientalism has been advanced through her endeavour.

72. Abu-Lughod makes a promising start in this direction by taking on the category of 'culture' itself. She argues that cultural difference is a problematic concept with connotations of homogeneity, coherence and timelessness. One way to subvert this category would be to focus on the

particular and work with the concrete, daily realities of individuals. This inevitably highlights similarities as well as differences and restores flux, contradiction and agency to actors previously frozen in their 'difference'. Lila Abu-Lughod, 'Writing against culture' in Robin G. Fox (ed.) *Recapturing Anthropology: Working in the present* (Santa Fe: School of American Research Press, 1991).

73. The results of these attempts are, in fact, debatable. Lazreg, for instance, argues that terms like 'women of color' which have become established in the United States actually reinscribe the very social relations they purport to combat. Marnia Lazreg, *The Eloquence of Silence* (New York and London: Routledge, 1994).

74. Marnia Lazreg, 'Feminism and difference: the perils of writing as a woman on women in Algeria', *Feminist Studies*, vol. 14, no. 1, 1988: 81–107.

75. Judith E. Tucker, 'The Arab family in history: "Otherness" and the study of the family' in Tucker (ed.), *Arab Women*.

Gender, Discourse and Ideology in Iranian Studies: Towards a New Scholarship

Joanna de Groot

The last fifteen years have seen significant transformations in Iranian studies. The Iranian revolution and the development of the Islamic Republic in Iran have re-directed much established research and writing on Iran in several ways. Focus on the events of the 1970s and 1980s has exerted a pull on scholarly attention both towards a specific temporal emphasis on contemporary/ recent history, and towards a concern with politico-ideological phenomena. Emphasis on themes such as the role of religious discourse and practice and on what some see as a 'crisis of modernity' in Iran has converged interestingly with a general turn in social and historical studies towards the cultural and the discursive, and with critiques of the notion of modernity.

In parallel to these developments we may note the cautious, partial, but undeniable engagement of some practitioners of Iranian studies with the newly dynamic field of gender and feminist scholarship which has grown up over the last two decades or so. The term 'parallel' is used advisedly, since it is my contention that, as with other fields of social and historical enquiry, work on women and gender issues is rarely *integrated* into the mainstream of Iranian studies. Whereas in the context of gender and women's studies I would emphasize the importance of cross-cultural approaches and avoidance of ethnocentrism for their continued success and relevance, my intention here is to make the case for the centrality of gender awareness within Iranian studies as a whole. I shall approach the argument through a critical assessment both of feminist scholarship and of writing on modern Iran, focusing on key examples within each field. My intention is to open up debate with suggestions about potentially fruitful areas for gender scholarship, and by emphasizing the need for Iranian studies *in general* to become gendered conceptually, methodologically and empirically rather than just 'adding on' gender as a discrete optional element in the field.

Developments in Gender Scholarship

The emergence of women's studies over the last fifteen years or so, and the more recent emphasis on gender, has involved three major initiatives designed to challenge, extend and transform existing gender-blind, masculinist scholarship. The first of these is a project of *recuperation*, in which issues, persons and materials which have largely been hidden, marginalized or overlooked are now being studied and analysed. Thus the production of historical and contemporary accounts of women's economic role, of sexual behaviour as a political question, or of gender roles and definitions as part of religious discourse or cultural representation is linked to the discovery or re-discovery of evidence and topics for investigation which fill gaps or open up new areas of study.[1] The second initiative is a project of *redefinition* in which new accounts of, say, women's economic role, involve new concepts of the nature of 'work', just as new accounts of male/female relations in marriage, household or child-rearing involve new concepts of 'the family'. Research and analysis have revealed the need not merely to accept new information about cultural or material or political life, but to re-think the categories in which economic activity, social relations or cultural practices are understood.[2] The third initiative is a project of *transformation* in which the actual frameworks of social, historical and cultural analysis are being challenged and altered in order to rectify their gender-blindness. This is a matter not merely of re-defining particular aspects of experience (politics, work, creativity, ideology), but of re-shaping the general categories and assumptions upon which much existing discussion of those areas are based, ranging from concepts of 'public' and 'private' to the notion of 'society' itself.[3]

Such projects are of course open to challenge, and fraught with contradictions and problems; but this has stimulated a whole range of new scholarship among both their supporters and their detractors, whether in social history, development studies or cultural analysis. Sexual divisions of labour, conflicts of interest between men and women in families or political movements, and the cultural construction of sexuality and gender identity are now established as significant areas of enquiry and debate for historians, social scientists and literary critics. However, the development of this scholarship has not gone unopposed, not only by those who deny the need for the intellectual innovations involved but also by those who point out the cultural limitations of the project. Some of the severest criticisms of the new gender-aware scholarship concern its ethnocentrism and tendency to generalize from the specific experiences of Western societies, referring both to the ethnic-cultural diversity of British or American society and also to the very different histories and structures of societies elsewhere.[4] Such criticisms have in turn stimulated the growth of a new genre of scholarly work exploring the interactions of gender, race and the history of world systems.[5]

Thus the emphasis of research and writing about women and gender questions shifted from critical engagement with the prevalent liberal or Marxist frameworks of scholarship during the 1970s towards greater concern with cross-cultural comparisons and exploration of issues concerning non-Western societies during the 1980s. Initially discussions of gender focused on its relationship to class structures, to socio-economic development in Western Europe and North America since the eighteenth century, and to political and cultural life in those areas during that period.[6] Latterly such discussions have involved the exploration of themes like the material involvement of so-called 'Third World' women in the world system, the interaction of gender politics with anti-colonial, post-colonial and liberation politics, and the relationship of gender to race, imperialism and cultural diversity.[7] This has not only made the whole area of gender scholarship more complex and varied, but also shaped its continuing engagement with the gender-resistant ideas and practices still prevalent in scholarly activity generally. Investigation and theorization of the structure and history of patriarchal systems, forms of gender power, and the links between violence, sexuality and domination, are now proceeding within a framework which attempts to take account of these new elements (with varying degrees of success).[8]

Gender Studies and Scholarship on Iran

It is in the context of these developments that I wish to consider the potential contribution of gender awareness to the study of Iran. I shall proceed from an examination of available texts which are founded on an understanding of the importance of this issue to discuss possible future directions, and to argue for the central relevance of systematic efforts to overcome gender-blindness in Iranian studies. A useful starting point is to look at some of the existing work dealing with gender matters in the context of Iran, work which reflects some but, as will be seen, not all aspects of recent gender scholarship. On the one hand there have been a number of studies which add accounts of gender and women to the body of work on contemporary Iran. These range from socio-anthropological micro-studies of rural, urban or nomadic communities to more general accounts of women's role in political or legal contexts. It is interesting to note the relative absence of general, as opposed to specific, studies of gender or women in an economic context, with the exception of brief accounts in Nashat and Jacqz or the recent work of Moghadam.[9] While there has been some recuperation of the material activities and experiences of women in *particular* situations, there is a significant absence of holistically gendered accounts of material life in Iran or of general syntheses or analyses of women, gender and economic life.

On the other hand there has been a series of quite extended discussions of gender and women in the ideological and political context of the Iranian revolution. These have focused both on the nature of women's involvement in the anti-Shah movement, and on the place of gender issues in that movement and in the dominant religious ideology, as well as on the treatment of gender, sexuality and women in the Islamic Republic. They have moved from works written in the context of disillusionment with what has seemed to many of the authors of these works to be the lost opportunities, failed promises, or misleading aspects of the revolutionary era, to more developed, reflective explorations of gender aspects of culture and politics.

Looking first at substantive studies on contemporary Iran we may understand them as examples of the first, recuperative initiative discussed earlier. Many existing studies, whether of particular communities or of general issues, tended both to concentrate on male experiences, ideas, activities and interests, and to treat the social and cultural construction of differences and relations between the sexes (i.e. gender) as unproblematic. These two characteristics reinforce one another, since it is only when female experience, interests etc. are given equal consideration with those of males that gender will emerge as an issue requiring social, political and cultural investigation and analysis. In the absence of such developments the scholars working on Iranian topics dealt with male/female roles and relationships within gender-blind and ethno-centric sociological discourses on 'the family', or anthropological discourses on 'kinship', or politico-economic discourses on 'modernization'. If male/female differences became a scholarly issue they tended to be located as 'natural' or given within particular contexts or communities, or as components of more general processes of change in labour markets, education or urbanization associated with 'modernity'.[10] Even more typically, many major social and political studies of modern Iran simply failed to take up these issues seriously at all. It was the emergence of gender-aware scholars and scholarship in fields other than Iranian studies, rather than internal developments within them, which provided models and conditions for a new approach.

Attempts at recuperation

As has been the case with other areas of study, the first impetus of those pursuing more gender-aware forms of scholarship has been to establish a descriptive basis which will 'recover' women and gender empirically from previous neglect. It is significant that much of this work has taken the form of micro studies of particular communities using the 'hands-on' methodologies of participant observation and personal interviewing. Such approaches not only overcome undoubted problems of the absence or inaccessibility of other categories of evidence (official, historical, national), but also are particularly appropriate for the exploration of issues concerning gender and women. Many of these issues only appear in the course of direct observations of and discussions with the subjects of study which are uniquely capable of revealing the construction of gender by tapping into the fabric of social and cultural values, practices, rules, institutions (and silences) which shape gender roles, gender relations and gender power. Thus the evocations of gender in an urban setting by Bauer, Gulick and Betteridge, in rural situations by Friedl and Hegland, or 'tribal' contexts as with Tapper and Beck break the silence on this topic both by providing information and description but also by challenging some of the obstacles to gender studies.[11]

A somewhat different category of specific scholarship has focused on themes of the legal regulation and status of women and gender relations. Deriving in part from the Orientalist and modernization views of law as a cultural agent articulating 'Islamic' values or a means to assist or impede 'progress', this approach to gender and women has received further impetus with the new concern to explicate the 1979 Revolution and Islamic Republic. Thus the work of Fischer and Pakizegi can be connected to the later work of Afshar and Haeri by virtue of their choice of a legal perspective on social control, social change and cultural discourses around gender.[12] It is worth noting, however, that for Fischer, as for Haeri, the use of anthropological methods and strategies is central to the impact and argument of their work, and that the connections which are being made link legal views and practices to cultural, political and ideological aspects of gender rather than to material aspects. In this sense the study of those views and practices has served to reinforce the trends which have affected Iranian studies generally, and paradoxically to maintain the 'separateness' of gender as a 'topic for investigation', while also signalling its importance in the construction of social and political change and power relations.

In addition to such contributions to Iranian gender scholarship there have also been attempts to look at aspects of this field from more general points of view. Notable among these is Sanasarian's *Women's Rights Movement in Iran*, part of which deals with the contemporary situation. Interestingly it owes more to the conventions and assumptions of political science and established liberal thought on gender questions as 'equality' questions (as shown by the title) than to recent developments in the study of women's movements or political activity generally.[13] The collection of studies on *Women and the Family in Iran* also seems to aim for some general overview of its subject although its anthology format and use of individual case studies do not wholly accord with that objective. Again, many of the studies (and the editorial 'line') owe more to social science conventions about 'women in the family' than to the cogent critiques and re-evaluation of such conventions from the perspective of gender interests, gender power or gender conflict.[14] The real contribution of such work has been in the breaking of silence on the subjects in question, and the signalling both of bodies of information and of areas for future investigation, as is also true of some of the brief legal surveys dealing with women and gender. It should be noted that the very limitations of this empiricist and recuperative placing of such issues on the agenda of Iranian studies stimulate critiques which, as will be seen, can move the discourse to a more developed stage.

Interrogating Islam

However, any account of the state of gender discourse in Iranian studies would be incomplete without discussion of the major body of work which has developed in relation to the politics and ideology of the Iranian revolution and Islamic Republic. The heightened visibility of women in the anti-Shah movement, and the considerable attention given to sexuality and gender roles in the ideological debate and propaganda of various protagonists of the 'revolution', and in post-revolutionary politics, provided a clear incentive for researchers and theorists concerned with the interactions of gender, ideology and politics. Moreover this occurred at a time when feminist activity and theory (the main sources of creative approaches to gender) were becoming more interesting both to political activists outside Western Europe/North America and to intellectuals concerned with the 'Third World' and the Middle East. The outcome was a series of studies in the early 1980s which explored the politicization of women and gender, the contradictions in religious ideology and women's situation, and the role of these developments as the political climate in Iran shifted from innovation and insurrection towards consolidation, conformity and repression.[15]

Certain important themes recur in these studies. The obvious centrality of religious ideologies, religious leadership and religious organizations in the present period, and the specific attention paid by such ideologies to gender and sexuality has given rise both to expanded expositions of themes and variations in established Shi'i theory and practice on those questions, and to investigations of its relevance to the actual situation and outlook of Iranian women. Such discussions have frequently been linked to discussion of the failure of other political views or groupings either to challenge the dominant religious/fundamentalist trend or to engage effectively with gender issues or a female constituency.[16] Another recurring concern is with the lack of historical social or political autonomy for gender-based and/or feminist movements. This is sometimes attributed to the impact of a repressive state, sometimes to limitations in the social and educational development of Iranians, sometimes to the alien or irrelevant character of feminist politics and ideas.[17] Whatever priority is given to these various explanations, there is something of a consensus, firstly that the problem is an ideological/political one, and secondly that the period 1978–81 offered an opportunity for developing challenges to the dominant gender order which has now passed.

Much might be said in detail about the insights and problems offered by the studies under discussion, but in the context of this chapter it seems more useful to raise general issues which can form the basis of further discussion. Firstly, it should be noted that the developing concern with gender and with women has largely remained separated from broad treatments of the Iranian revolution and the Islamic Republic. That is to say that, if mentioned at all, those subjects remained in a ghetto of 'specialist' concern rather than informing any general analysis of contemporary Iran; the repression of women's interests is treated as simply an 'instance' of the repressive activity or character of the state and religious/fundamentalist para-statal agencies (Pasdaran etc.); the discussion and regulation of sexual behaviour is an instance of fundamentalist ideology at work; the decline of women's political activity is an instance of the failure of all oppositional politics to make headway. In any case the interest of many commentators has shifted from the broad political scene to the 'high politics' of in-fighting among the Islamic Republican Party/government leadership, or to the conduct and implications of the Iran–Iraq war. One can see here the effects both of resistance within conventional masculinist scholarship and of the way in which the discussions of gender and women have themselves been presented merely as *particular* cases. Since those discussions did not aspire to be hegemonic within the discourse, they did not create conceptual or theoretical means to move gender to a more central position within established scholarly perceptions of contemporary Iran.

Thus, much existing gender scholarship has been located within other discourses (political science, development studies, neo-Marxism), accepting as its parameters what Iranian women accepted within their political activities during the revolution — that gender interests are subordinate or irrelevant to other social, religious or national political interests. As several works on women in the Iranian revolution note, there are persuasive explanations, both historical and structural, for this situation. These range from the long history of general political oppression at various periods and the chauvinism of most twentieth-century political movements, to the cultural and social confinement of women shaped by lack of opportunity for education, employment or personal independence, and lack of any influential historic legacy of gender or

woman-centred politics. However, while analysis of such phenomena is vital for any adequate account of the role of gender in
Iranian politics (or lack of it), there often seems to be a slippage
from discussing this as an issue *within* Iranian studies to accepting
it as a valid framework for those studies themselves. While many
authors clearly argue for the importance of autonomous woman-
centred political and social involvement relevant to the specifics of
the Iranian situation they seem less clear about the need for a
similar transformation of Iranian studies. The development of a
discourse and programme for such a transformation is a vital task
for gender-sensitive scholarship in the field. It requires not only
the incorporation of an empirical account of gender within the
mainstream of Iranian studies, but also the alteration of the
existing theoretical and methodological constructs within which
they are pursued.

Directions for New Scholarship

While attempts to challenge the androcentrism of Iranian studies
at that level are not much in evidence, there have been interesting
developments of the discussions of gender, women, Islam and
politics which explore their interactions in much richer, more
complex ways than previously. The work of Afsaneh Najmabadi,
who significantly works both on women/gender issues and on
other socio-political themes ranging from rural social change to
discourse analyses of nationalism, is a case in point. Her most
recent discussion positions 'women-and-politics' much closer to a
general analysis of evolving political cultures, interests and power
relations in Iran and deals with it as *part* of the map of forces
making up a complex historical process of state formation, political
agenda setting and social change.[18] Rather than accepting an
ancillary place for questions of sexuality, gender equality and
gender politics, this treatment constitutes them as central elements
within the realm of politics, shaping a mainstream history of
conflict and change around projects of modernity. In this sense it
begins to re-shape a gendered account of politics, history and
culture in Iran in ways congruent to my own work on the earlier
part of the century, and that of Paidar on women in the political
discourses of the whole period.[19]

Not only does scholarly concern with gender need to leave its
ghetto and generally inform studies of contemporary Iran, but it

also needs to broaden the study of gender from its current location in the realm of politics and ideology. It is not of course surprising that current scholarship has concentrated on the phenomena of female political involvement and the use of gender issues (segregation, veiling, regulation of sexuality, marriage etc.) by the Islamic regime, nor should that scholarship be denigrated. Iranian circumstances during the last decade logically push such matters to the forefront, and studies of these issues have attempted to locate them within the complex totality of social and historical development.[20] However, the contingent urgency of explicating political and ideological aspects of gender in contemporary Iran which informs much writing on gender, has to some extent under-privileged more wide-ranging accounts of the *material* construction of gender both before and after the Iranian Revolution, and I would argue that this situation needs to be altered. This should not be read as advocacy of some sort of economic reductionism which would narrowly interpret gender politics in terms of the organization of labour and production, or of old-fashioned con-cepts of class, but rather as a suggestion that the whole range of social relations and experiences in production and reproduction should be analysed from a gendered viewpoint. Such an analysis would locate the politics and ideology of gender within a history of recent transformations of family, employment and material culture (e.g. the creation of specific conditions of women's experi-ence of migration, wage-labour, education, care-work). Here the community-based studies referred to earlier provide both material for a more general analysis and also the beginnings of a paradigm which integrates material change, culture and politics in a struc-tured totality of gender analysis.

The recent work of Erika Friedl exemplifies some of the poten-tial in this approach. Her presentation of the lives of rural women through narratives which foreground their own active constructions of their situation rather than hers, closely connecting material with cultural processes and practices in a dynamic whole, works at several levels; it offers a degree of empowerment and validation to her subjects which is in the best tradition of feminist scholarship with its commitment to challenge the silencing of women and the unreal separation of lived experience from the mental processing and analysis of experience; it is also in that tradition of social/historical scholarship which 'listens' rather than condescends to those being studied, and acknowledges their human agency as 'thinking' as well as 'doing' persons; it illustrates the potential both of reflexive anthropology and discourse analysis to come together. Similarly Friedl's contribution to Keddie and Baron's volume makes an imaginative critique of conventional analyses of women's relationships to so-called 'public' as opposed to 'private' space through a creative and powerful integration of material and cultural analysis. Here we can see a real move from descriptive to analytical presentation of women and gender relations which conveys a sense of gendered totality.[21]

The notion of gendered totality as the appropriate framework for contemporary Iranian studies would be liberating not only for studies of gender in the Iranian context, but also for the analysis of Iranian society as a whole. Here one can draw on feminist scholarship with its arguments for the integration of gender awareness into the mainstream of social and cultural study, so that analyses of literary activity, family life or divisions of labour incorporate concepts of gender difference, conflicting gender interests and unequal gender power. Studies which implement this insight in a variety of contexts have shown that gender-aware scholarship can illumine the study of class structures, of Third World development, and of creative arts in various cultures. They have shown how transformations in production and labour processes whether local, national or international involve sex/gender differences and how the social and cultural constructions of gender in family, media or community are essential aspects of the historical process, as are challenges to those constructions. This also applies to the development of the African–American women's studies, to the new approaches to social history and popular culture, and to work in colonial and post-colonial studies.[22] These are all instances where questions of gender in politics and/or the politics of gender are connected to a range of material and cultural developments and to the concept of gender as a crucial element in the social whole.

Broadening the Agenda

However, if such approaches are to be applied to the study of contemporary Iran it is important to be aware of problems and limitations as well as of the insights and advantages offered by feminist scholarship. As was noted earlier, many concepts developed within that scholarship are highly Euro-centric in character. Accounts of the construction of gender identities and sexuality have over-privileged the experience of Western societies since the eighteenth century; the development of theories of patriarchy, whether as 'father-right' or 'male power', has tended to a universalism and ahistoricality which obscures their potential for useful application to a wide range of specific social and historical circumstances; the debates over the interactions of gender, family, class experiences and structures have concentrated excessively on processes most typical of Western industrial societies.

These biases have been challenged, at least at a political level, in the writing by and about women of colour in Western societies as well as in work on women in non-Western societies and on gender in relation to imperialism and racism.[23] However, as Kandiyoti notes, such critiques have not always been accompanied either by systematic attempts to apply feminist scholarship to, for example, Middle Eastern societies, or conversely by full use of information and experience in those societies to critique that scholarship.[24] This can be seen particularly clearly in discussions of gender in relation to Islam, where the Orientalist scholarly legacy has led both to a failure to separate the role of religion from other shared social or historical influences, and to a universalization of 'the Islamic' regardless of its specific social, political or historical contexts. The problematic nature of such a treatment is especially obvious in the context of Iranian studies, granted the very particular forms of Islam in Iran and their intersection with popular culture, ethnic identity and patterns of political opposition.

Detailed expositions of both the ideological and the institutional (legal) influence of religion on gender roles and relations since 1979 have tended to focus on the textual and public aspects of this phenomenon (Qur'anic prescription, speeches of Khomeini and other leading *ulama*, activities of government agencies, Pasdaran etc.). A notable exception is Haeri's treatment of *mut'a* marriage which combines textual with social investigation.[25] Clearly these forms of legitimation and enforcement of gender rules and control of women are very significant, but such formal and prescriptive religious influences need to be related to the more informal, communal or family-based aspects of gender regulation for any full appreciation of gender dynamics. The work of Bauer and Betteridge, like that of Friedl, suggests how such issues can be explored, allowing us to understand not only the socio-cultural basis of religious ideology, but also the interrelation between ideology, its cultural expression, and the circumstances of people's lives. The 'organization of consent' to religiously sanctioned gender rules is facilitated not just by the institutions of state or faith, but also within the intimate and everyday experience of civil society in which the authority of kin, the influence of neighbours and communities, and individual internalization reproduce dominant cultural values and practices regarding gender. Moreover, that consent is reinforced by other influences; the pressures generated by urban migration create needs to adapt and re-affirm gender divisions and gender roles in new economic and social situations; the collision of competing values and images of respectability and femininity has sharpened popular discourse over rules of sexual, marital and family conduct; the impact of public propaganda which is populist, nationalistic and anti-Western, as well as religious, connects gender rules not only to Muslim loyalties and practices but also to self-assertion against foreign influence and elite decadence.[26]

It is the development of themes such as these that will fill out the accounts of the gender dimension in popular culture which informed the anti-Shah movement and subsequent acquiescence with post-revolutionary orthodoxy. Since most existing studies on these questions relate to the earlier 1980s, further work needs to take account of processes which have developed since then, following the lead of Paidar's work which links analysis of the earlier period to a discussion of developments during the last decade.[27]

Indeed, a sense of process and historicity in the study of gender in Iranian society is another important antidote to the Orientalist or social structuralist approaches which emphasize timeless 'Islamic' influences or static social analysis at the expense of dynamic and interactive approaches to this topic. The significance of the high profile given to sexual morality and codes of gender behaviour over the last decade in Iran needs to be understood in the context both of changes (both short and long-term) in every sphere of life, and also in terms of the dynamics of political crisis itself. Just as the upheavals of the Constitutional Revolution and the movements of the 1940s opened spaces for gender politics, so the crisis of the Pahlavi regime and the processes involved in consolidating the Islamic Republic also placed the issue on the political/ideological agenda. This should be seen not merely as a historical opportunity for advocates of particular gender rules to politicize their case, but equally as a situation in which gender is

appropriate as a *medium of discourse* through which a whole range
of debates on state, society and legitimacy can be articulated.

As has been shown in the case of both Turkish and Egyptian
nationalism, images of gender and femininity can become central
representations of the politics of cultural autonomy, progress/
modernity or anti-imperialism.[28] Rather than seeing the 'emancipation' of women or the 'restoration' of proper morality and/or
authentic custom in gender behaviour simply as items on a
modernist, nationalist or fundamentalist agenda, they are better
understood as powerful signifiers in the main discourses of fundamentalism, nationalism or modernity. The proper integration of
gender into studies of contemporary Iran requires adequate investigation and explanation of the gendered character and gendered
history of political practice and ideology as a whole, a task advanced by Najmabadi's current work. On the one hand this would
involve exploration of the symbolic and signifying role of gender
questions within political movements or arguments, following the
example of Fischer's discussion of the politics of veiling, to construct accounts of both the neglect of and the attention to gender
which transcend mechanistic explanation.[29] On the other hand it
would involve analysis of the relationship between masculine
identity and perceptions of legitimate authority, social or national
emancipation and cultural authenticity. Such analysis needs to
acknowledge the gendered nature of these perceptions and the
interpenetration of languages of male power and masculinity with
languages of popular, religious or national power, along the lines
of existing accounts of gender aspects of Black Power politics in
the USA, or of responses to colonialism developed by Lata Mani
and the 'Subaltern Studies' school.[30]

However, as has been pointed out, although gender presents
itself as a political and ideological issue in contemporary Iran, it
is also a social and material issue. It is not clear, for example, how
far ideological considerations about women's employment now
outweigh the demand for women's labour, notably in service work,
particularly domestic services, growth in which was a significant
feature of the 1970s. Equally it would be interesting to pursue the
discussion of women's changing role in rural communities opened
up in the work of Friedl and Hegland, or to look at the impact,
if any, of war conditions upon the family life (with its gender
divisions) of the urban poor. As Kandiyoti has suggested in the
Turkish case, ideological controls on gender and women interact

with a whole range of strategies for managing both cultural and material aspects of gender in the family and the community, and further consideration of this interaction in contemporary Iran would be a valuable contribution to social and gender studies.[31] The available evidence that popular awareness of the gender dimensions of social respectability also contains important elements of class and prestige awareness needs further analysis. While much existing scholarship on class/gender questions refers to circumstances different from, and perhaps irrelevant to, the Iranian situation, it does offer paradigms of a broad material analysis of differing social relations to power, production and property in which both elements (and others like ethnicity and age) play a role.[32]

By confronting these paradigms with the specifities of Iranian society it would be possible to develop accounts of the material aspects of gender in society based not on global or ethno-centric generalizations but on a vigorous comparative evaluation of concepts and theories of gender and class. While the macro-scale conceptualization of Mies' work on patriarchy and accumulation offers a stimulating, if controversial, global framework and narrative, it cannot fully incorporate such a specific evaluation of particular social and historical experience.[33] The onset of the Islamic Republic has not diminished the need for such work on gender in the Iranian context.

It is perhaps by the use of a rigorous comparative approach that appropriate and effective connections between the Iranian situation and the general body of gender scholarship can be established. Various studies of the socio-cultural construction, control and representation of gender roles and relations in the Mediterranean basin (north and south, east and west) suggest that while religious ideology contributes a significant element, there are other considerations which intersect and interact with particular religious influences. Common themes of the sexual aspect of honour-and-shame in family or community, of the demands of particular forms of rural production, or of dependency on markets, on sexual divisions of labour, or of state intervention in legal and educational spheres, transcend the religious and cultural divisions which also inform gender in society. Without reducing the discussion to bland generalization, such approaches can offer a focused method of comparison and remind us that family property interests, status in local communities, and their impact on marriage, economic

activity or child care, may well be more significant constituents of
gender than religion or ideology alone.[34] Clearly there are serious
substantive problems in investigating such issues in Iran at present,
but where there is genuine recognition of their importance, there
will also be incentives to make the most of what material is
available in order to explore them.

If the development of gender studies of contemporary Iran can
be advanced through the creative tension between general concepts and theories, comparative investigation and the specificities
of Iranian society, it can also benefit from exploration of the
contradictions within the dominant structures and culture. It is all
too easy to give an account of gender issues which emphasizes the
continuing subordination of women and hegemonic character of
the prevailing ideology at the expense of comprehending elements
of conflict and resistance. On the one hand, the 1979 Revolution
simultaneously mobilized women in the name of popular anti-
Shah, anti-American 'Islamic' politics and asserted male power
and authority as central aspects of those politics. As Mahjub's
1980 interview with a young woman supporter of Khomeini shows,
elements of submission to the patriarchal view of Islam can co-
exist with a strong sense of self-worth and self-definition within
the ideology. So she argues that the veil should be worn as a mark
of decency, but also that an Islam which denies her the right to
political activity or education is not the 'real' Islam, and she feels
confident to criticize her own father as well as unbelievers or 'bad'
Muslims.[35] Such sentiments are explicated in Paidar's treatment in
this volume of Islamist feminists in Iran. One is reminded of
Victorian feminist engagement with and subversion of Evangelical
gender restrictions, turning religion around to empower their challenge to subordination, although Sakineh does not even have the
privilege of middle-class socialization to bolster her self-assertion
as they did. Other studies of women's response to 'Islamic' ideology and politics also reveal a complex web of acquiescence and
criticism, pragmatic accommodation and sharp reservations of
dissent.[36] These realities should show us that any simplistic picture
of 'victims' and 'oppressors' cannot do justice to the dialectics of
gender in contemporary Iran.

This essay has merely opened up a range of options which
would allow scholars to enrich and correct the partial/biased
character of conventional Iranian studies by addressing and appre-
ciating the gender dimensions of Iranian society and culture. The

specificities of gender history should be articulated in their full social/historical context through appropriate investigation, conceptualization and analysis, just as that context should be clarified and demystified by the use of a comparative approach which critiques as well as drawing on existing gender scholarship. Since male experience and activity is conventionally presented as the gender*less* 'human' norm, appreciation of gender requires both due attention to their female equivalents and re-evaluation of *men* as *gendered* subjects. On this basis it will be possible to develop a clear sense of the complexities and contradictions of gender roles, gender relations and gender power. Above all I would contend that these projects are not so much an optional addition to a list of 'topics' but an essential requisite for the development of viable and legitimate Iranian studies as such.

Notes

1. See as classic examples Sheila Rowbotham, *Hidden from History* (London, 1973) or Louise Tilly and Joan Scott, *Women, Work and Family* (London, 1978) for history; Rayna Reiter, *Towards an Anthropology of Women* (New York, 1975) and Henrietta Moore, *Feminism and Anthropology* (Oxford, 1988) for anthropology; Alison Jaggar, *Feminist Politics and Human Nature* (Totowa, 1983) for philosophy; Roszika Parker and Griselda Pollock, *Old Mistresses* (London, 1981) or Toril Moi, *Sexual Textual Politics* (London, 1983) for cultural studies; Diana Leonard Barker and Sheila Allan (eds), *Sexual Divisions and Society* (London, 1976) and *Dependence and Exploitation in Work and Marriage* (London, 1976) for sociology.

2. See for example Veronica Beechey, 'On patriarchy', *Feminist Review* 4/5 (1979); Lorenne Clark and Lynda Lange (eds), *The Sexism of Social and Political Theory* (Toronto, 1979); Sylvia Walby, *Patriarchy at Work* (London, 1989); Michelle Barrett, *Women's Oppression Today* (London, 1980).

3. Carol Pateman, *The Sexual Contract* (London, 1988); Elizabeth Grosz and Carol Pateman (eds), *Feminist Challenges* (Sydney/London, 1986); Sylvia Walby, *Theorising Patriarchy* (London, 1989).

4. See bell hooks *Ain't I a Woman? Black women and feminism* (Boston, 1981); *Feminist Theory* (Boston, 1984) and *Talking Back* (Boston, 1989); Elizabeth Spelman, *Unessential Woman* (Boston, 1988); Valerie Amos and Pratibha Parmar, 'Challenging imperial feminism', *Feminist Review* 17 (1984); Arthur Brittan and Mary Maynard, *Sexism, Racism and Oppression* (London, 1984).

5. Angela Davis, *Women, Race and Class* (London, 1981); Jacqueline Jones, *Labour of Love, Labour of Sorrow* (New York, 1985); Kate Young, Carol Wollkovitz and Roslyn McCullagh, *Of Marriage and the Market* (London,

1981); Lourdes Beneria and Gita Sen, 'Accumulation, reproduction and women's role in economic development', *Signs* (1981); J Scott et al., *Household and the World Economy* (London, 1984); Barbara Rogers, *The Domestication of Women* (London, 1980).

6. See for example Tilly and Scott, *Women, Work and Family*; Jane Rendall, *The Origins of Modern Feminism* (London, 1985); Annette Kuhn and Anne-Marie Wolpe, *Feminism and Materialism* (London, 1978); Cynthia Cockburn, *Brothers* (London, 1983).

7. Examples are Maria Mies, *The Lace-makers of Narsapur* (London, 1982); Kumari Jayawardena, *Feminism and Nationalism in the Third World* (London, 1986); Floya Anthias and Nira Yuval-Davis (eds), *Women, Nation, State* (London, 1989); Deniz Kandiyoti (ed.), *Women, Islam and the State* (London, 1991); Gita Sen and Cheryl Crown, *Development Crises and Alternative Visions* (New York, 1987); Gayatri Spivak, *In Other Worlds* (London, 1987); Sarah Graham-Brown, *Images of Women* (London, 1988); Joanna de Groot, ' "Sex" and "race"; the construction of language and image in the 19th century' in Susan Mendus and Jane Rendall (eds), *Sexuality and Subordination* (London, 1989); Catherine Hall, *White, Male, and Middle Class* (London, 1992).

8. See Caroline Ramazanoglu, *Feminism and the Contradictions of Oppression* (London, 1989); Deniz Kandiyoti, 'Emancipated but unliberated', *Feminist Studies* 13 (1987), and 'Bargaining with patriarchy', *Gender and Society* 2/3 (1988); Fatmagul Berktay, 'Looking from the "other" side; is cultural relativism the way out?', and Joanna de Groot and Mary Maynard, 'Facing the 1990s; problems and perspectives for women's studies', both in Joanna de Groot and Mary Maynard (eds), *Women's Studies in the 1990s: Doing things differently* (London, 1993).

9. S. Kaveh-Mirani, 'Social and economic change in the role of women 1956–1978' in Guity Nashat (ed.), *Women and Revolution in Iran* (Colorado, 1983), and Hamideh Sedghi and Ahmed Ashraf, 'The role of women in Iranian development' in Jacqueline Jacqz (ed.), *Iran, Past, Present and Future* (1976) are both fairly brief; see also more recently Valentine Moghadam, 'Women's work and ideology in the Islamic Republic', *International Review of Middle East Studies*, 20 (1988); Haleh Afshar, 'The position of women in an Iranian village' in Haleh Afshar (ed.), *Women, Work and Ideology in the Third World* (London, 1985) and A. Aghajanian, 'The impact of development on the status of women: a district level analysis in Iran', *Journal of Developing Societies*, 8 (1991).

10. See Sedghi and Ashraf, 'The role of women in Iranian development'; Jacqueline Touba, 'Sex role differentiation in Iranian families', *Journal of Marriage and the Family* (1975), and 'The relationship between urbanization and the changing status of women in Iran', *Iranian Studies* (1972); Asghar Fathi, 'Social integration in the traditional Iranian family' in Asghar Fathi (ed.), *Women and the Family in Iran* (Leiden, 1985).

11. Janet Bauer, 'Demographic change, women, and the family in a migrant neighbourhood of Tehran' in Fathi (ed.), *Women and the Family in Iran*, and 'Poor women and social consciousness in revolutionary Iran' in Nashat (ed.), *Women and Revolution in Iran*; John and Margaret Gulick, 'The domestic social environment of women and girls in Isfahan' in Lois Beck and Nikki Keddie (eds), *Women in the Muslim World* (Cambridge, Mass., 1978) and 'Migrant and native women in the Iranian city of Isfahan', *Anthropology Quarterly* 49 (1976); Anne Betteridge. 'To veil or not to veil?' in Nashat (ed.), *Women and Revolution*; Erica Friedl, 'Women and the division of labour in an Iranian village', *MERIP Reports*, 95 (1981) and 'State, ideology and village women', in Nashat (ed.), *Women and Revolution*, and 'The dynamics of women's spheres of action in rural Iran' in Nikki Keddie and Beth Baron (eds), *Women in Middle Eastern History* (London/New Haven, 1991) and *Women of Deh Koh* (Washington 1989); Mary Hegland, 'The village women of Aliabad and the Iranian Revolution', *RIPEH* (1981) and 'Aliabad women; revolution as religious activity' in Nashat (ed.), *Women and Revolution* and 'Iranian village women; how do they cope?', *RIPEH* (1979); Nancy Tapper, 'The women's sub-society among the Shahsevan nomads of Iran' in Beck and Keddie, *Women in the Muslim World* and 'Matrons and mistresses; woman and boundaries in two Middle Eastern societies', *Archives Européenes de Sociologie* 21 (1980); Lois Beck, 'Women among Qashqai nomad pastoralists' in Beck and Keddie, *Women in the Muslim World* and 'The religious lives of Muslim women' in Jane Smith (ed.), *Women in Contemporary Muslim Societies* (1981).

12. Michael Fischer, 'On changing the concept and position of Persian women' and Behnaz Pakizegi, 'Legal and social positions of Iranian women' both in Beck and Keddie, *Women in the Muslim World*; A. and Adèle Ferdows, 'Women in Shi'i *fiqh*' in Nashat (ed.), *Women and Revolution*; Haleh Afshar, 'Women, state and ideology in Iran', *Third World Quarterly* 7/2 (1985) and 'The legal, social, and political position of women in Iran', *International Journal of the Sociology of Law* 13, 1985; Shahla Haeri, 'The institution of *mut'a* marriage in Iran' in Nashat (ed.), *Women and Revolution* and *Law of Desire* (Syracuse, N.Y. and London, 1989).

13. Eliz Sanasarian, *The Women's Rights Movement in Iran* (New York, 1982).

14. Asghar Fathi (ed.), *Women and the Family in Iran* (Leiden, 1985) is a good example.

15. These include Farah Azari (ed.), *Women of Iran: the conflict with fundamentalist Islam* (London, 1983); Azar Tabari and Nahid Yeganeh (eds), *In the Shadow of Islam* (London, 1982); Nashat (ed.), *Women and Revolution*. See also Haleh Afshar in Tabari and Yeganeh, *In the Shadow*, and 'Behind the veil: the public and private faces of Khomeini's policies on Iranian women' in Bina Agarwal (ed.) *Structures of Patriarchy* (London, 1988); 'Women, Marriage and the state in Iran' in Haleh Afshar (ed.) *Women,*

48 JOANNA DE GROOT

State and Ideology (London, 1987); 'The emancipation struggles in Iran' in Haleh Afshar (ed.), *Women, Survival and Development in the Third World* (London, 1991); 'Women and reproduction in Iran' in Anthias and Yuval-Davis (eds), *Woman, Nation, State*; Parvin Paidar in this volume.

16. See for example Tabari and Yeganeh, *In the Shadow*, pp. 16–17, 24, 27 and Haleh Afshar in Azari (ed.), *Women of Iran*, pp. 158–61.

17. See Sanasarian (ed.), *Women's Rights Movement*; S. Bahar in Azari (ed.), *Women of Iran*, pp. 170, 180–1, 148–55; Yeganeh, *In the Shadow*, pp. 35, 37–8, 69–71.

18. Afsaneh Najmabadi, 'Hazards of modernity and morality: women, state and ideology in contemporary Iran' in Kandiyoti (ed.), *Women, Islam and the State*, and 'Iran's turn to Islam', *Middle East Journal* 41 (1987) and 'The de-politicisation of a rentier state' in H. Beblawi and G. Luciani (eds), *The Arab State* (London, 1987); see also Najmabadi's *Land Reform and Social Change in Iran* (1987); also 'Zanha-yi millet: women or wives of the nation?' *Iranian Studies*, vol. 26 Spring 1994: and 'Veiled discourse–unveiled bodies', *Feminist Studies*, vol. 19, no. 3, Fall 1993.

19. Joanna de Groot, 'The dialectics of gender: women, men and political discourses in Iran c.1890–1930', *Gender and History* 5/2 (1993); Parvin Paidar, *Women and the Political Process in Twentieth-century Iran* (Cambridge, 1995) and her chapter in this volume.

20. See e.g. Ervand Abrahamian, *Iran between Two Revolutions* (Princeton, 1982); M. Parsa, *Social Origins of the Iranian Revolution* (New Brunswick and London, 1989); Said Amir Arjomand, *The Turban for the Crown* (Oxford and New York, 1988).

21. Friedl, *Women of Deh Koh* and 'The dynamics of women's sphere of action' in Keddie and Baron (eds), *Women in Middle Eastern History*.

22. Impressive examples are Leonore Davidoff and Catherine Hall, *Family Fortunes: men and women of the middle class c.1780–1850* (London, 1987); Mary Poovey, *Uneven Developments: the ideological work of gender in Victorian England* (London, 1989); Hazel Carby, *Reconstructing Womanhood* (Oxford/New York, 1987); Kandiyoti, *Women Islam and the State* and 'Islam and patriarchy' in Keddie and Baron (eds), *Women in Middle Eastern History*.

23. Carby, *Reconstructing Womanhood*; Leila Ahmed, *Women and Gender in Islam* (New Haven/London, 1992); Margaret Strobel and Nupar Chaudhuri (eds), *Western Women and Imperialism* (Indiana, 1992); Vron Ware, *Beyond the Pale* (London, 1992); Antoinette Burton, *Burdens of History* (Chapel Hill, 1995).

24. Deniz Kandiyoti, 'Islam and patriarchy' in Keddie and Baron (eds), *Women in Middle Eastern History*, and 'Emancipated but unliberated'.

25. Haeri, *Law of Desire*.

26. Bauer, Betteridge and Friedl in Nashat (ed.), *Women and Revolution*; see also Ann Betteridge 'The controversial vows of Iranian women' in N. Falk and R. Gross (eds), *Unspoken Worlds: Women's religious lives in non-Western Cultures* (San Fransisco, 1980); Joanna de Groot, 'The formation and

reformation of popular movements in Iran' in Kenneth Brown, Sami Zubaida et al. (eds), *The State, Urban Crises and Social Movements in the Middle East* (Paris, 1989).

27. Paidar, *Women and the Political Process*, and in this volume.

28. Deniz Kandiyoti, 'Slave girls, temptresses and comrades', *Feminist Issues* 8/1 (1988) and 'Women as metaphor in the Turkish novel' in Brown and Zubaida (eds), *State, Urban Crises and Social Movements* and 'Islam nationalism and women in Turkey' in Kandiyoti (ed.), *Women, Islam and the State*; Margot Badran, 'Dual liberation; feminism and nationalism in Egypt', *Feminist Issues*, 8/1 (1988); Thomas Philipp, 'Feminism in nationalist politics in Egypt' in Beck and Keddie (eds), *Women in the Muslim World*; Juan Cole, 'Feminism, class, and Islam in turn of the century Egypt', *International Journal of Middle East Studies* 13/4 (1981); Beth Baron 'Mothers, morality, and nationalism in pre-1919 Egypt' in Rashid Khalidi et al. (eds), *The Origins of Arab Nationalism* (Chicago, 1991) and 'The construction of national honour in Egypt', *Gender and History* 5/2 (1993).

29. Michael Fischer, *Iran: From religious dispute to revolution* (Cambridge, Mass., 1981).

30. See the work of bell hooks; Patricia Collins, *Black Feminist Thought* (Boston 1990); Franz Fanon, *Black Faces, White Masks* (New York, 1962); Lata Mani 'Contentious traditions: the debate on *sati* in colonial India' in Kum Kum Sangari and Sudesh Vaid (eds), *Recasting Women: Essays in colonial history* (New Delhi, 1989); Gayatri Spivak, 'Can the subaltern speak? Reflections on widow sacrifice', *Wedge* 7/8 (1985). For Iran see the work of de Groot and Najmabadi cited above in notes 18, 19.

31. Kandiyoti, 'Emancipated but unliberated' and 'Islam and patriarchy'.

32. See for example Barbara Taylor, *Eve and the New Jerusalem* (London, 1983); Davidoff and Hall, *Family Fortunes*; Judith Walkowitz, *Prostitution and Victorian Society* (Cambridge, 1980); Ava Baron (ed.), *Engendering Work*.

33. Contrast Maria Mies, *Patriarchy and Accumulation on a World Scale* (London, 1985) with, for example, Samita Sen, 'Motherhood and mother-craft: gender and nationalism in Bengal', *Gender and History* 5/2 (1993) or Donald Quataert, 'Ottoman women, households and textile manufacturing 1800–1914' in Keddie and Baron (eds), *Women in Middle Eastern History*.

34. Monique Gadant (ed.), *Women of the Mediterranean* (London, 1986) or David Gilmore (ed.), *Honour and Shame and the Unity of the Mediterranean* (Washington, DC, 1987).

35. In Gadant, *Women of the Mediterranean*, pp. 59–71.

36. See the Bauer and Friedl articles in Nashat (ed), *Women and Revolution* and English comparisons available in Taylor, *Eve and the New Jerusalem*; Gail Malmgreen (ed.), *Religion in the Lives of English Women* (London, 1986); Philippa Levine, *Victorian Feminism* (London, 1987); Rendall, *Origins of Modern Feminism*; Bonnie Smith, *Ladies of the Leisure Class* (Princeton, 1981). To these add French and American comparisons.

Feminism and Islam in Iran

Parvin Paidar

Feminism(s)[1] in the Middle East and their articulations with Islam have attracted substantial interest in recent years. This chapter will focus on the interaction between feminism and Islam in Iran. It will trace, in general terms, the development of feminism in that country and the ways in which it has interacted with Islam at various historical moments since the turn of the century. While in recent decades feminisms in the Arab Middle East by and large make reference to utopian Islam(s) to defend women's rights, in Iran the interaction between feminism and Islam has taken place in the context of a militant Shi'i state which claims to have implemented 'true Islam'. The contrast between these contexts may provide a useful contribution to an understanding of the interaction between feminism and Islam in various Middle Eastern contexts.

The approach adopted in this chapter emanates from the view that far from being an optional extra, gender is situated at the heart of political discourses in Iran. Indeed, any political discourse aiming at the social re-organization of Iranian society has necessarily entailed a redefinition of gender relations and of women's position in society. Therefore, this chapter will place the interaction between Islam and feminism in the broader context of political process in twentieth-century Iran.

Early Twentieth-Century Nationalist Feminism

In tracing the historical development of feminism in relation to Islam, a natural starting point would be the constitutional movement of the early twentieth century, since this was the context within which the 'woman question' was first explicitly raised in Iran.

The Constitutional Revolution of 1906–11 took place against the background of Western intrusion and the rise of nationalism.[2]

It revolved around the demand for constitutional monarchy to
curb the power of the monarch in favour of the power of parliament and the rule of law on the one hand, and to protect Iran's
national interests in the face of Western economic and political
intervention on the other. It rested upon a diverse urban alliance
which included merchants, traders, land owners, secular intellectuals and the Shi'i clergy.[3] The importance of the constitutional
movement for women was in the creation of a particular vision of
modern Iran. The concept of modernity encapsulated justice,
democracy, independence and women's emancipation. The movement created a conceptual link between national independence
and progress and women's emancipation. It constructed women
as social actors for the first time and facilitated the formation of
a network of women's rights activists which gradually developed
into a loosely formed women's movement.[4]

Since the very idea of women's emancipation was grounded in
the need for national progress, women activists prioritized the
general developmental gains implicit in the improvement of
women's position. The main demands of the women's movement
included education and the abolition of practices such as seclusion
and early marriage, which were regarded as serious impediments
to women's contribution to national development. The way in
which women's emancipation became associated with national
progress during the constitutional period, created a generic link
between feminism and nationalism which has shaped the course
of Iranian feminism ever since. This has had at least two consequences. First, it has made it impossible to talk about the interaction between feminism and Islam without taking into account
the links between Islam and nationalism. Second, this has been
one of the main reasons why individualistic types of feminism
based on women's personal experience and individual choice, a
stance commonly associated with feminism in the West, have not
developed in Iran.

The type of nationalism that developed in Iran in the first half
of the century was on the whole secular. It was constructed as an
alternative discourse, as Islam was associated with traditionalism
and backwardness. During the constitutional period, secular intellectuals played an important role in constructing concepts such as
constitutionalism, nationalism, modernity and women's emancipation. Amongst these intellectuals were Mirza Fath Ali who
expressed a deep admiration for pre-Islamic Iran and Dehkhoda

who advised women to drive the mollahs out of their lives. Some of these intellectuals were professed atheists such as Akhundzadeh, Christians such as Malkam Khan, or converts to Babism such as Mirza Agha Khan Kermani.[5] Babism was of course one of the main indigenous sources of inspiration for women's emancipation at the turn of the century[6] since one of its female protagonists Tahereh Qorrat ol-Eyn took off her veil in public and challenged the *ulama* (Muslim clergy) to debate women's position with her.[7]

From the beginning of this century, then, the concept of women's emancipation became grounded in concepts associated with nationalism and modernity and in ideas inspired by pre-Islamic Iran, new religions such as Babism and the influence of the West. However, the debate on women was conducted in a way which avoided outright confrontation with religion. Feminists of this period complained against social conservatism rather than Islam as such. For example, Bibi Khanum Astarabadi argued that 'The obstacle to women's emancipation is not Islam but the male interest to preserve his privileges. If men decide to give women freedom, they would bend every rule to find an Islamic justification for it.' [8]

Although the secular debate on women avoided outright opposition to Islam, nevertheless the expression of ideas inspired by non-Islamic sources was considered to be a serious threat by many Shi'i clerics. The Shi'i establishment focused on opposing the practical steps taken to emancipate women. For example, the opening of each new school for women was accompanied by a campaign by local mollahs to close it down.[9] This is not to say that the clergy were united on the question of women's education —on the contrary. Those supporting the Constitution, such as Ayatollah Tabataba'i, allowed their daughters to attend school, while anti-constitutionalist clerics such as Nuri opposed it and tried to stop it by inciting mob attacks on schools. Sheikh Fazlollah believed that 'If we allow girls and handsome boys to go to school, corruption will spread in society like a plague.'[10] However, the Shi'i establishment did not make a serious attempt to present an intellectual challenge to, or defence of, women's emancipation. I have not come across any serious or substantial Islamic apologia or Islamic reformist ideas on women in Iran in the early twentieth century, comparable to those of Mohammed Abduh and Qasim Amin in Egypt at the end of the nineteenth century.

So while women's protests against subordination were conducted within an acceptable cultural framework which avoided overt criticism of Islam, the main point of reference for these women was secular nationalism. The secular nature of early twentieth-century feminism was strengthened further in the post-Constitutional period as a result of two particular developments; the rise of socialism and establishment of the Bolshevik state across the border in Russia[11] and the emergence of the state as an agent of social reform.

The establishment of a strong socialist state in a neighbouring country and the resulting rise of socialism amongst Iranian intellectuals helped the post-Constitutional women's movement to develop its own independent identity and become more organized and diverse at the same time. In the first half of the century, whenever freedom of expression prevailed, different factions of the movement forged alliances and created support networks with the political parties of their choice. The socialist women's organizations tended to be the most active ones. Many women activists of this period came from either clerical families, such as Sediqeh Dowlata-badi, or from the aristocracy, such as Mohtaram Eskandari. The main issues of the campaign on women included education, veiling, seclusion, child marriage, polygamy and political rights.[12]

The emergence of the state as an agent of social reform was an even more important development affecting Iranian feminism in the early part of the century. The state established by Reza Shah Pahlavi in 1925 had a nationalist outlook and valorized pre-Islamic Iran. It set out to transform Iran from a dependent, backward society to a modern, independent nation-state and as a result the state became the initiator and implementor of social reform and assumed responsibility for the health, welfare and education of the population, at least in rhetoric.[13]

Statist Feminism and the Rise of Cultural Nationalism in Mid Twentieth-Century Iran

However, in imposing reform on women's position, Reza Shah's state adopted a forceful and centralist approach and ended an era of women's independent activities by creating a state-sponsored women's organization to lead the way on women's emancipation. The measures proclaimed included compulsory unveiling, free education and, potentially, the creation of new employment opportunities. These measures had been demanded by many constitutionalists and feminists since the turn of the century, and by implementing them the state took the initiative on women's issues away from independent socialists, liberal nationalists and feminists.[14] With a silent Shi'i establishment, co-opted nationalism, a suppressed socialist movement, and a partly co-opted, partly suppressed women's movement, the only voice allowed on behalf of women was that of the state.

The second Pahlavi state, established in 1941 after the abdication of Reza Shah in favour of his son, Mohammad Reza Shah, continued the same pattern of modernization, co-option and political suppression. The initial period of constitutional rule under the Shah resulted in the formation of a short-lived liberal nationalist government by Mohammad Mosaddeq who led a coalition of nationalist forces. The nationalist government, however, did not have a specific gender agenda and its half-hearted attempt to introduce a new electoral bill which included enfranchisement for women failed. A CIA-sponsored coup in 1953 against Mosaddeq restored the Shah's autocratic rule.[15] The post-coup period of 1960s and 1970s witnessed heightened suppression of most autonomous political groupings. But it also resulted in further state initiatives on women's rights. The campaign for political rights conducted by prominent feminists, such as Fatemeh Sayyah, had some success despite substantial opposition by the clergy.

The 1960s and 1970s also saw the growth of cultural nationalism and Islamic modernism.[16] This occasioned a shift in the interaction between feminism, nationalism and Islam. The rise of cultural nationalism as a new political force closely associated with Islam resulted in the Shi'i establishment reclaiming lost moral ground on women and family issues as a result of several new developments.

First, on the religious front, after the death in 1961 of Ayatollah Borujerdi, the highest Shi'i authority of his time, a group of high-ranking clerics shared similar high status and gained their own followers.[17] These Ayatollahs, including Khomeini, published and circulated widely their religious opinions on a broad range of issues, including women and the family. These religious views about women's position found political expression in a campaign by an Iranian version of the Muslim Brotherhood in the 1960s which presented a new fundamentalist defence of the Shi'i *shari'a* on women.[18]

Second, on the political front, reformist clerics such as Ayatollah Motahhari and lay religious radicals such as Ali Shari'ati articulated new models of Muslim womanhood for Iranian women.

The ideas of Shari'ati were adopted by the Mojahedin-e Khalq, who represented the Islamic tendency within the Marxist-Leninist guerrilla movement of the 1960s and 1970s which led a crusade against the Pahlavi state.[19]

The success of these new Islamic trends in regaining the initiative on women and the family was due to both ideological and political factors. The Pahlavi state's unwillingness to introduce fundamental changes on women's position within the family enabled the Shi'i establishment to regain the initiative fairly easily. Both Reza Shah and Mohammad Reza Shah focused their reforms on the civic aspects of women's roles as opposed to the familial ones. Despite tremendous opposition by the Shi'i establishment, both Pahlavi regimes pushed forward with women's education, unveiling and de-segregation, while the reforms that they carried out on the family remained relatively limited. Pahlavi reforms did not go beyond a codification of traditional Shi'i law on women and family as part of the Civil Code of 1936, and an attempt to limit arbitrary male power in the family through the introduction of Family Protection Laws in 1967 and 1975. These limitations were due not so much to clerical opposition as to deeper concerns about the wider implications of granting women real power and independence within the family. The Pahlavi regimes opposed women's independence in the family and their independent presence in the public sphere, and this influenced the logic behind state-sponsored women's organizations which made sure that women's lives inside and outside the home remained under the control of male guardians. This strengthened the clergy's ideological hold over matters concerning women and the family, which was translated so effectively into a successful political campaign by the Shi'i movement during the 1970s.

However, the existence of new Shi'i ideas on women would not by itself have affected feminism in Iran if the political developments of the 1970s had not pushed them to the forefront.[20] The rise of Shi'ism as a serious modern political movement in the context of anti-Shah politics became a major factor in the adoption of Shi'i ideas on women. The revolutionary context provided fertile ground for the first serious confrontation of secular feminisms (such as statist and socialist feminism) by political Islam. For the first time, Islamic activism became a serious political option for Iranian women, and many women from the younger generation who were totally alienated from state feminism took it up. The Pahlavi state's claim to be liberating women was politically untenable; the nationalist opposition was not able to present an alternative gender policy to that of the state and the socialist alternative only attracted a small minority of women. As a result, the campaign on women's issues became the preserve of the Islamic opposition.

The Islamic campaign on women included appeals to reject 'Westernization' and the exploitation of women as 'sex objects' which was seen as the consequence of Iran's economic and cultural dependence on the West. Instead, women were urged to embrace the new Shi'i model of womanhood which represented 'authenticity' and 'independence' and emphasized women's dual role as mothers and revolutionaries.[21] This found credence with large groups among both religious and secular women because it promised political freedom, economic equality, social justice, cultural integrity and personal fulfilment. It facilitated women's massive participation in the Revolution of 1979.[22]

The contrast between women's participation in the 1979 Revolution and the earlier Constitutional Revolution could not be sharper, and was rooted in the different interactions between Islam and feminism in each revolutionary period. The 1979 Revolution was the second attempt in this century, apart from the brief Mosaddeq period, to redefine and change existing relations between the state and Western powers with the aim of establishing independence and democracy in Iran. But while the former revolutionary movement aimed to achieve this through emulation of the Western liberal model of society, the latter aimed to achieve it by constructing an 'indigenous' and 'authentic' Islamic model of society in Iran. Moreover, while the flavour of the first revolutionary discourse was that of a liberal nationalism associated with secularism, the second revolved around a cultural nationalism associated with Islam.

In summary, Iranian feminism was essentially secular until the rise of Shi'i modernism in the 1970s. It was only then that the new trend of Islamist feminism (gender activism within an Islamic framework) joined other feminisms in Iran.

Islamist Feminism and State Policy in the Islamic Republic

Let us now consider the development of Islamist feminism under the Islamic Republic. After the establishment of the Islamic

Republic, the new constitution gave a prominent place to women, defining them as mothers and citizens. It stressed that the establishment of an Islamic nation was dependent on the Islamization of women and constructed the ideal Islamic woman in opposition to Western values on womanhood. The constitution attempted to create harmony between the Islamic family and nation by advocating a set of patriarchal relations to strengthen male control over women in the family on the one hand, and granting women the right to be active citizens on the other.[23]

The link between nationalism and Islam was crucial in determining the gender policies of the Islamic Republic. After the Islamic Republic settled into a theocracy, nationalism as a mobilizing force was transformed and re-defined. The state attempted this by constructing nationalism as synonymous with anti-imperialism on the one hand, and replacing nationalism with Islam as the main mass mobilization force on the other.[24] The new alliance between Islam and anti-imperialism, for which historical precedents existed in Iran, constituted the cornerstone of the Islamization policy of the state. The context of revolutionary populism, anti-imperialism, the effects of a war economy and struggle for state power between Islamic factions determined which concepts and ideas on women were defined as 'Islamic' and which ones as 'un-Islamic'. The result was a significant reversal of the history of clerical opposition to women's participation in politics. For example, the same clerics who had in the 1960s objected to women's enfranchisement on religious grounds were in the 1980s prepared to grant women the right to vote in the name of Islam.

With regard to women's social role, the Islamic Republic formulated policies on women's education, employment and political participation to ensure the continuation of women's mass support. Women's political participation was approved because it legitimized the state's Islamization policies and created an image of popular support and stability internally and internationally. These policies, however, were based on the premise that women's presence outside the home had to be accompanied with a process of de-sexualization of male-female interaction to protect the Islamic family and nation from its harmful moral consequences. A number of policies were developed to ensure this.

First, the protection of the family required the strengthening of male privilege through the Islamization of the Iranian household. The Family Protection Law was abolished and the Civil Code of

1936 was reinstated. This meant that the modest safeguards created for women in matters of divorce, marriage, child custody and abortion were all revoked overnight. Second, an extensive policy of gender segregation and compulsory *hejab* (head cover and loose clothes) for women was implemented. Third, measures were introduced in order to police the integrity of the family. These measures became known as the 'anti-corruption crusade', with a broad definition of corruption covering any social mixing between men and women as well as adultery, homosexuality, consumption of drugs and alcohol, gambling and a whole range of leisure activities.[25]

Having thus structured the social role of women, the postrevolutionary Islamic state encouraged the development of an Islamic women's movement to counter the threat posed by secular feminism. The spontaneous movement of secular women to defend their rights against the Islamic state was crushed and secular feminism was driven into exile.[26] Like preceding secular regimes, the Islamic state has ensured that the women's movement remained under tight state control. Different factions of the state and the state-sponsored revolutionary organizations attempted to harness women's tremendous mobilization potential by creating platforms for Islamic women activists.

The hard-line factions of the state took control of women's mass mobilization by organizing mass rallies in support of state Islamization and against the secular and Islamic opposition. Women's mass support was also manipulated in relation to two other areas of importance to the survival of the state—elections and the war against Iraq.

While women from the lower classes provided the mass support that the Islamic regime needed, Islamic women leaders became involved in philanthropic, religious, and feminist activities. Many of the state-funded welfare agencies, health and education centres, charities and foundations were run by women. Women who managed such organizations often came from clerical families and were well-connected within the circle of Islamic leadership.

A third category of Islamist women took up feminist activities under the patronage of the moderate factions of the state. The Women's Society of the Islamic Revolution (WSIR) was founded soon after the Revolution by a group of women to preserve and build upon the revolutionary demand for a culturally authentic gender identity. The popular, formerly pro-Pahlavi, women's magazine, *Zan-e Ruz* (Woman of Today), was taken over by an editorial board of Islamic feminists and transformed into a popular Islamic women's magazine. These women tended to be highly educated, often with doctorates from Western universities, and professionals in various fields. Their activities included not only publishing women's magazines, but also running women's organizations and formulating Islamic policies on women.

During the post-revolutionary transitional period of 1979–81, Islamist feminists drew their support from the religious faction of the Provisional Government and later, in some cases, the office of President Banisadr. The same period witnessed the forceful imposition of a hasty Islamization programme by Ayatollah Khomeini. This went against the views of Islamist feminists who wanted instead a long-term, gradualist Islamization programme based on educating women about the values of Islam.

Islamist feminists set out to create a vision of the 'ideal Islamic society' and the role of women in it. The idealization of the future Islamic society entailed a critique of the past and the present. The Islamist feminist theory of women's oppression and liberation was constructed in opposition to 'traditional Islam'. 'True Islam', according to Islamic feminists, transcended the 'traditional, deviatory and colonized Islam' in relation to women.[27] The failures of traditional Islam were seen as rooted in male-dominated culture and distorted interpretations of Islamic laws.

Ayatollah Khomeini's Islamization measures received coded criticisms from the Islamist feminists. Azam Taleghani and Zahra Rahnavard, two well-known activists, warned the authorities about the negative effects of forcing women to wear *hejab*. They proposed that the Islamic dress code should not be made specific to women but that both men and women should be required to wear simple and decent clothing which covers the body in a non-arousing, modest fashion.[28] On the Islamic Republic's policy of excluding women from the judiciary, Islamic feminists argued that 'women's emotionality is not an acceptable ground for their exclusion from passing judgement,' and said that 'Muslim women should be able to take their legal problems to female judges as much as possible, just as they take their medical problems to female doctors.'

Despite the enormous enthusiasm of these women and initial expectation that they would make a major contribution to the Islamic Republic's gender policies, Islamist feminists were marginalized by the hard-line factions of the post-revolutionary government. Ayatollah Khomeini's tendency to ignore voices of moderation, together with repressive state policies, resulted in the radicalization of the feminist strand of the Islamist women's movement. During the politically extremist years of 1981–87 the voice of Islamic feminism was thus silenced almost completely.

This took place in the context of a diversity of Islamist opinions, political power struggles, political repression, ideological control, economic stagnation, war and international isolation. These developments affected the ability of the state to establish coherent policies or ensure their effective implementation. Although the general framework of state policies on women was defined by opposition to the Pahlavi regime and 'alien Western values', actual policies of Islamization were formulated in a heterogeneous and *ad hoc* manner by a variety of agents with different and sometimes conflicting interests.[29] The way this affected women can be seen in the pattern of their education and employment in this period. Although strongly encouraged in official rhetoric, in reality women's education and employment suffered from contradictory policies, the imposition of gender quotas and support for male dominance, combined with lack of co-ordination between the multiple centres of decision-making and lack of financial resources. Nevertheless, although the opportunities available to women were reduced, Islamization policies and mismanagement did not stop women's participation in education and employment.[30]

The state also failed to deliver 'Islamic justice' in relation to women's position within the family. Women had been promised support for their 'natural' rights and roles. They were to receive economic and legal protection from the Islamic state and its male representatives in the home. In return, women were expected to prove their credentials as obedient wives, self-sacrificing mothers and active citizens.[31] However, this equation failed to work in the actual political and economic circumstances of the Islamic Republic. On the contrary, measures such as the strengthening of male authority in the family not only failed to increase women's protection, but actually resulted in the reduction of women's familial rights and the deterioration of their material condition.[32] The Islamic Republic may have given its female supporters the opportunity for popular political participation and a sense of righteousness and self-worth, but it seriously undermined women's position within the family and restricted their human rights.

All this gave greater credence to the cause of Islamist feminism.

To survive during particularly repressive periods, Islamist feminists tried to be as non-controversial as possible, and in doing so they colluded extensively with state attacks on women's rights. The degree of loyalty to the state expected from Islamist feminists proved to be much higher than that expected from the pro-state feminists of the Pahlavi era. Despite this, the extremist years had a maturing effect on Islamic feminists. They realized that unless they established an autonomous existence and spoke out against state policy, women would continue to get a raw deal despite the state's claim to represent 'true Islam'. Thus, a small but vocal Islamist feminist opposition re-established itself in the late 1980s.

Since the late 1980s, Islamist feminists have been able to campaign for women's rights in a much more open and direct manner than before. They have also proved more successful in pressurizing the policy-makers to revise earlier restrictions on women's legal rights and to consider positive proposals for greater rights for women within an Islamic framework. The issues on which they have campaigned have included family, education, employment, political participation and *hejab*. On education and employment, which seem to be the most sophisticated and successful issues on which Islamic feminists have campaigned, discriminatory practices towards women have been scrutinized and proposals made for their eradication. One important achievement in this area has been the lifting of restrictions that had been placed on women's entry to technical, scientific and medical fields soon after the Revolution.

Campaigns on the family have focused on improving the balance of power between men and women in the family. The emphasis has been put on the concept of 'partnership between husband and wife' as opposed to the concept of 'male guardianship', which is the basis of the Civil Code. Islamist feminists have protested against the failure of state policy to 'facilitate the growth of women's talents and personality', 'preserve their rights in the sacred institution of family', 'protect the rights of unprotected women' and 'remove obstacles in the way of women's participation in economic, social and political activities.'[33] The policies advocated include state remuneration for housewives and unmarried women, monogamy, automatic custody rights for mothers, protection against divorce without the wife's consent, the right of wives to half the family assets, and women's rights to undertake education, employment or travel without the consent of husbands or other male guardians.

However, despite achieving relative independence for their movement and having some success in persuading policy-makers to extend women's rights, Islamist women leaders have on the whole had limited opportunities to take on decision-making roles and have had a hard time gaining authority or influence in the Islamic polity. Only a handful have entered the Islamic parliament or the government. Eleven elections during the first decade of the Islamic Republic have produced in total only six women representatives in parliament, an even more tokenist minority than in the Pahlavi era.

The presence of women in the government has been even more limited. Women are barred from the presidency, and post-revolutionary cabinets have not yet included a woman minister. Women have only been appointed in a consultative capacity and allocated seats in consultative committees set up in the parliament and various ministries. They have also been included in the delegations to international conferences. More recently a woman has been assigned as the adviser to the president of the Republic on women's issues.

Conclusion

This incursion into contemporary Iranian history demonstrates that gender issues have been at the heart of Iranian politics and that they have undergone complex and sometimes paradoxical transformations. This has been nowhere more apparent than under the Islamic Republic. Indeed, the transformation of Islamist feminism from post-Revolutionary idealism to realism and pragmatism of the late 1980s has been remarkable. This being the case it is no longer inconceivable to envisage strategic alliances between Iranian strands of secular and Islamist feminisms on women's rights issues. The frames of reference of the two traditions of gender activism are, of course, very different. Iranian Islamist feminism is theoretically rooted in cultural relativism and politically rooted in anti-imperialism, while the direction taken by Iranian secular feminism in exile in the last decade has been largely universalist, anti-religious and increasingly individualistic.

However, the severity and material reality of the problems faced by Iranian women have reduced the importance of these ideological differences. To illustrate this point, it will be useful to compare the experiences of feminists campaigning to improve family laws in the Pahlavi era with those under the Islamic Republic. It took about forty years for secular feminists of the Pahlavi era to change the family law from the Civil Code of 1936 to the Family Protection Law of 1975. In 1979, it took Ayatollah Khomeini one speech to demolish the Family Protection Law in a single blast; and since then it has taken Islamist feminists over twelve years to build it again bit by bit; the task has yet to be completed.

The same family laws which had been historically presented by the Pahlavi state as part of a process of secularization and which were opposed by the clergy as contrary to Islam and therefore demolished, are now being reinstated under the Islamic Republic. The difference does not seem to be in the Islamist or secular nature of the law but in the political priorities of the era. This has created a potential for co-operation and alliance amongst ideologically diverse feminisms. Old ideological enemies may turn into new political allies when it comes to resisting the onslaughts of male supremacy. Although these alliances may be fraught and fragile, they speak of Iranian women's will to act upon their gender interests.

Notes

1. The term 'feminism' will be used in this article in the broadest possible sense to accommodate any type of activism by women focusing on their gender interests within any political or ideological framework. I will refer to a number of different feminisms, such as Islamist feminism, secular feminism, state feminism, socialist feminism. This broad definition of 'feminism' is not intended to obscure the differences between 'feminism' and 'gender activism'. However, this article does not concern itself with the issue of whether or not the women's movements described here were 'feminist'. That is why it is justifiable to use 'feminism' and 'gender activism' synonymously in this particular context in order to emphasize the links between women's movements and political ideologies rather than the nature of women's activism.

2. Nikki Keddie, *Roots of Revolution* (New Haven and London: Yale University Press, 1981).

3. Ervand Abrahamian, *Iran Between Two Revolutions* (Princeton: Princeton University Press, 1982).

4. Mangol Bayat-Philip, 'Women and revolution in Iran' in Louise Beck and Nikki Keddie (eds), *Women in the Muslim World* (Cambridge, Mass.: Harvard University Press, 1978).

5. Bayat-Philip, 'Women and revolution'.

6. On Babism see Abbas Amanat, *Resurrection and Renewal: The making of the Babi movement in Iran 1844–1850* (Ithaca: Cornell University Press, 1989).

7. The word *ulama* means Islamic scholars. On Tahereh Qorrat ol-Eyn see Farzaneh Milani, *Veils and Words: The emerging voices of Iranian women writers* (Syracuse and London: Syracuse University Press and I.B.Tauris, 1992); also Amanat, *Resurrection and Renewal*.

8. Fereydun Adamiyat and Homa Nateq, *Afkar-e ejtema'i, siasi va eqtesadi dar asar-e montasher nashodeh-e dowran-e Qajar* (The social, political and economic thought of the Qajar period in unpublished documents) (Tehran: Kharazmi, 1978), pp. 20–7. On Bibi Khanum also see English translation and introduction by Afsaneh Najmabadi, *Ma'yib al-rijal* (Vices of men) (Chicago: Midland Press, 1992).

9. *Mollah* is a general term for lower-ranking clergy. On women's educational activities in this period and the *mollahs'* opposition to them see Eliz Sanasarian, *The Women's Rights Movement in Iran* (New York: Praeger, 1982).

10. Homa Nategh, 'Jang-e ferqeha dar enqelab-e mashrutiyat' (The battle of factions in the Constitutional Movement), *Alefba*, 3, p. 47.

11. Abrahamian, *Iran Between Two Revolutions*.

12. On women activists of this period see Badr ol-Moluk Bamdad, *From Darkness into Light: Women's emancipation in Iran*, edited and translated by F.R.C. Bagley (New York: Exposition, 1977).

13. On the Reza Shah period see Keddie, *Roots of Revolution*.

14. Afsaneh Najmabadi, 'Hazards of modernity and morality: women, state and ideology in contemporary Iran' in Deniz Kandiyoti (ed.), *Women, Islam and State* (London: Macmillan, 1991).

15. On the Mosaddeq era see James Bill and W. Roger Louis (eds), *Musaddiq, Iranian Nationalism, and Oil* (London: I.B.Tauris, 1988).

16. On cultural nationalism during this period see Houchang Chehabi, *Iranian Politics and Religious Modernism: The liberation movement of Iran under the Shah and Khomeini* (London: I.B.Tauris, 1990) and Sussan Siavoshi, *Liberal Nationalism in Iran: The failure of a movement* (Boulder Colorado: Westview Press, 1990)

17. On developments within Shi'i institutions see Shahrough Akhavi, *Religion and Politics in Contemporary Iran: Clergy-state relations in the Pahlavi period* (Albany, N.Y.: State University of New York Press, 1980).

18. The term *shari'a* refers to Islamic canonical law. On the Iranian equivalent of the Muslim Brotherhood see Adèle Ferdows, *Religion In Iranian Nationalism: A study of the Fadaiyan-i Islam*, unpublished Ph.D. Dissertation, 1967, University of Indiana.

19. For Shari'ati's most influential work on women see Ali Shari'ati, *Fatima is Fatima*. Translated by Leila Bakhtiar (Tehran, 1980). On the

Mojahedin see Ervand Abrahamian, *Radical Islam: The Iranian Mojahedin* (London: I.B.Tauris, 1989). On the revolutionizing of popular Islam in the 1970s see Michael Fischer, *Iran: From religious dispute to revolution* (Cambridge, Mass.: Harvard University Press, 1980).

20. On the transformation of Shi'ism into political ideology see Sami Zubaida, *Islam, the People and the State: Essays on political ideas and movements in the Middle East* (London: Routledge, 1989; Tauris, 1993).

21. See Afsaneh Najmabadi, 'Iran's turn to Islam: from modernism to a moral order' in *Middle East Journal*, vol. 4, no. 20, 1987; and Nahid Yeganeh, 'Sexuality and Shi'i social protest in Iran', in Juan Cole and Nikki Keddie (eds), *Shiism and Social Protest* (New Haven: Yale University Press, 1986).

22. On women's participation in the 1979 Revolution see Guity Nashat (ed.), *Women and Revolution in Iran* (Boulder Colorado: Westview Press, 1983); and Adèle Ferdows, 'Women and the Islamic Revolution' in *International Journal of Middle East Studies*, no. 5, 1983.

23. For a translation of and introduction to the constitution see Hamed Algar, *The Constitution of the Islamic Republic*, (Berkeley: Mizan Press, 1980).

24. See Nahid Yeganeh, 'Women, nationalism and Islam in contemporary political discourses in Iran' in *Feminist Review*, no. 44, Summer 1993.

25. For a selection of articles on early post-revolutionary Islamization see Azar Tabari and Nahid Yeganeh (eds), *In the Shadow of Islam: The women's movement in Iran* (London: Zed Books, 1982).

26. On the suppression of secular feminism see Kate Millet, *Going to Iran* (New York: Coward, McCann and Geoghegan, 1982)

27. See Fereshteh Hashemi, 'Women in an Islamic versus women in a Muslim view' in Tabari and Yeganeh (eds), *In the Shadow of Islam*.

28. On Ayatollah Khomeini's policy on *hejab* see Haleh Afshar, 'Behind the veil: the public and private faces of Khomeini's policies on Iranian women' in Bina Agarwal (ed.), *Structures of Patriarchy: The state, the community and the household* (London: Zed Books, 1988). On the Islamic feminist response to women's participation in the legal profession see Fereshteh Hashemi, 'Proposal for the legal revival of the rights of women' in Tabari and Yeganeh (eds), *In the Shadow of Islam*.

29. On social developments in the Islamic Republic see Shaul Bakhash, *The Reign of the Ayatollahs: Iran and the Islamic Revolution* (London: I.B.Tauris, 1984).

30. On women's education and employment in the Islamic Republic see the following works: Sahar Ghahreman,'The Islamic state's policy towards women's access to higher education and its socio-economic effects' in Nime*ye Digar: Iranian Women's Feminist Journal*, no. 7, 1988; Shahrzad Mojab, 'State control and women's resistance in Iranian universities' in *Nimeye Digar: Iranian Women's Feminist Journal*, no. 14, 1991; Valentine Moghadam 'Women, work and ideology in the Islamic Republic' in *International Journal of Middle East Studies*, vol. 20, 1988.

31. See Deniz Kandiyoti, 'Islam and patriarchy: a comparative perspective' in Nikki Keddie and Beth Baron (eds), *Women in Middle Eastern History* (New Haven and London: Yale University Press, 1992).

32. On the effect of polygamy on women see Shahla Haeri, *The Law of Desire* (London and Syracuse: I.B.Tauris and Syracuse University Press, 1989).

33. These quotes have been drawn from articles in the following Iranian magazines and newspapers in the course of 1979–89. *Zan-e Ruz* (a women's weekly magazine), *Zanan* (an Islamist women's weekly magazine), *Ettela'at* (daily newspaper), *Kayhan Hava'i* (weekly edition of a daily newspaper).

4

Gender Relations and Inheritance: Person, Power and Property in Palestine

Annelies Moors

In this chapter I will argue that a focus on gender as a relational concept may illuminate and transform our understanding of the relations between power and property which have been at the centre of debates in both history and anthropology. In the case of women and inheritance in the Muslim Middle East, much of the literature starts from the nature of the property involved. It is argued that the property rights of women are better protected in the case of real estate and movables than if agricultural land is involved (Pastner 1980). Authors working on Ottoman cities point out that women had more access to residential than to commercial or agricultural property (Jennings 1975; Gerber 1980; Marcus 1983). Those writing about rural areas state that women stand a better change of inheriting land if it is individually owned rather than collectively held (Layish 1975; Peters 1978).

Such materialist notions about the impact of the nature of property often tie in with concerns about the relationship between property and power. A major motivation in concentrating on women's access to property has been to counter claims about the particularly 'depressed' (Gerber 1980: 231) or 'despised' (Jennings 1975: 53) position of women in Muslim societies. Taking women's access to property as indicative of a relatively autonomous position such studies assume a direct, positive and often reciprocal link between property and power.

When I started working on women's access to property in Palestine such notions also informed my approach. Discussions with Palestinian women, however, disclosed that inheriting property could have widely divergent meanings, calling into question both the centrality of the nature of the property involved and the assumed direct relation between property and power. In this paper I will, inspired by Whitehead (1984), shift the focus from the property involved to the specific positions women take up or find themselves in, and from property as a material resource to property as a social relation. In order to do so I will examine the strategies women adopt with respect to inheriting property, which vary from renouncing their rights to actively claiming their share.

This account is based on fieldwork in the 1980s in Jabal Nablus, Palestine, both in the city of Nablus itself and in al-Balad, the fictive name of a small village in the region, the inhabitants of which were previously dependent on dry-farming and goatherding and more recently on remittances from migrant male wage-labour. Only the most common cases of women inheriting, that is as daughters and widows, will be discussed. Before turning to inheritance practices, a short summary of the legal context is presented.

Law, Property and Inheritance

The nature of property is emphasized not only in academic writing but also, albeit in a different way, in the legal system itself. In the Jabal Nablus region, as in other areas which were once part of the Ottoman Empire, succession is regulated through two different legal systems. Property held in full ownership (*mulk*), such as urban real estate, buildings, vineyards, orchards and movables, is inherited in accordance with the Islamic law of succession. Most agricultural land (but not plantations) is not *mulk* but *miri* land to which individuals could acquire rights of usufruct and possession, but with ultimate ownership remaining vested in the state. This right of possession is also inheritable, but in this case a secular law of succession is applied.

Within these two systems it is not the nature of the property, but gender, marital status, kin relation and the presence of contending heirs which determine inheritance rights. In Islamic law a widow is entitled to a fixed share of one-eighth of her late husband's estate if he had children (not necessarily by her) and one-quarter if not. A widower in a similar situation would take twice as much: one-quarter and one-half of his wife's estate respectively. Daughters receive a fixed share if the deceased has no sons: one daughter is entitled to half the estate, two or more sharing two-thirds of it. Thus, if a man dies without leaving sons, a considerable part of the estate goes to his male agnates, usually his brothers. If, on the other hand, there are sons, these are the first heirs and daughters turn into agnatic heirs, entrusted with one-half the share of a son.

While *mulk* property is inherited according to Islamic law, a very different law of succession is applied to *miri* land: the Ottoman *intiqal* (succession) system. Its main principles are gender equality and distribution of the estate on the basis of generations. The major heirs are the children of the deceased, and if there are none, the parents, with the surviving spouse receiving one-quarter of the estate if the deceased had children and one-half if there were none.

Daughters with Brothers: Problems of Dependence and the Pleasures of Identification

Among small property owners the most striking common feature of women's inheritance stories was and is that daughters with brothers generally refrain from claiming their inheritance share. In the village of al-Balad the legal differentation between *mulk* and *miri* property is of little practical importance to women. Neither is women's exclusion from inheriting linked to the presence of more collective forms of landownership. As far back as people remember there was very little communal land, yet women commonly do not claim their share.

Women themselves point out that it is not the nature of the (landed) property, but rather that of kin relations which is relevant. When in the 1920s Granqvist, an anthropologist working in Artas, a village near Bethlehem, asked why a woman does not take her share of inheritance, the answer was 'But then she would have no more rights to her father's house' (1935: 256). Women in al-Balad in the 1980s by and large expressed very similar sentiments, underlining that a daughter reaffirms and strengthens her ties with her brothers by leaving her share to them, ties that are of great importance to women. After marriage women tend to continue to identify with their own kin and feel a special closeness to their natal household, as well as being dependent on their male kin for their economic security. By not claiming her share, a woman enhances the status of her brothers and by implication her own and accentuates their obligations towards her. As women's inheritance rights are widely recognized, refraining from claiming these rights places a brother in a position of obligation *vis-à-vis* his sister. If, on the other hand, a woman demands her share in the estate, her kinship ties with her brothers may well be disrupted irremediably and she may no longer be able to invoke their help and support. As the support she can count on from her own relatives usually influences her position in her husband's house, this simultaneously undermines her position *vis-à-vis* her husband and in-laws.

For similar reasons daughters of urban small property owners often did not and still do not claim their rights in their father's estate. With the family house and workshops seen as indicators of their long-established presence in the city, this property is not only central to the family's livelihood, but also has a strong symbolic meaning. In artisan households skills, tools and workshops are usually transmitted from father to son, and the house, often the only other type of property, is destined for the sons, their wives and children. For small metal workers, sweet makers, carpenters, shoemakers and so on, it is inconceivable to split up the property, nor is there sufficient cash available to 'buy out' the sisters. Like her rural counterpart, an urban daughter would often opt for the strategy of strengthening her brothers' position by renouncing her share in their favour, and she would do so for the very same reasons: identification with and dependence on her father's household. In fact until recently, with a stricter gendered division of labour in the city, women's economic dependence there was even greater.

Despite strong historical continuities and the great importance of relations with brothers, the conjugal relationship has become more accentuated through time. Writing about the 1920s Granqvist acknowledged that marriage was important for a woman, as unmarried women were an easy target for gossip, but emphasized that it was a brother who would protect and help her in time of need. After all, 'the husband is only a garment which a woman puts on or throws off again, or she herself can be "thrown off" by her husband, but the brother is the one who is always there' (Granqvist 1935: 253). Women in al-Balad in the 1980s, on the other hand, tended to place greater emphasis on the central role of husbands as providers. In response to my queries as to why women do not claim their inheritance share, they pointed out that their brothers need the land 'because they have to take care of their wives and children; women themselves can do without, as their husbands will provide for them.' Yet, even if they consider husbands as the main provider, they still recognize the importance of having a brother in times of hardship and only rarely take the risk of disrupting their kin relation by claiming property rights.

'Wealthy Women': Receiving Gifts

Daughters of small property owners often argue that they do not claim their share in their father's estate as there is little to divide and their brothers need what there is to be able to provide for their households. Does this mean that wealth makes it easier for women to receive their share?

To some extent this is, indeed, the case. It is true that among the wealthy, big merchants, high office holders, and large landowners productive property and real estate are also transmitted patrilineally and generally remain under male control. Still, in those households where sufficient assets are available, giving daughters a share in their father's estate is seen as enhancing the status of the family as a whole. So daughters are often allocated a share in the income from the property concerned. However, this may happen after a considerable lapse of time and daughters may well receive less than they are legally entitled to.

Moreover, those taking an active interest in their financial entitlements have to face the problem that it is not deemed proper for a woman to enquire about her father's estate. Khawla, for instance, a successful professional woman in her early forties, did not find it easy to realize her property rights. After her father, who had been a wholesale trader in cloth and a large landowner, died in the early 1950s, the property remained undivided. It was not until 30 years later, when her mother also died, that it was officially divided. By then Khawla had been married to a well-known businessman for over 15 years, had two teenage daughters, one of whom had a health problem, and had herself taken up professional employment.

When her father's estate was divided, three of her brothers and two sisters were still alive. In keeping with common practice her brothers made all the arrangements for the division of the estate. Khawla, motivated by her concern for the future of her daughters who, as she emphasized, would not have a brother to protect them, wanted to know what was going on, but found it difficult to ask. 'The majority, also the educated people, consider it a shame for a woman to inquire after her inheritance share. They say she is negligent of her brother (*bitqasir akhuha*). So my sisters remained silent, they were too shy to ask. But I was strong, and because I fought they also received their share.' Indeed, her brothers were displeased about their sister's inquisitiveness. As Khawla put it: 'I have inherited by fighting, not in court, but by telling them "I will not sign anything unless you show me everything." After all, they did not work hard for it, my father did and he left it for all of us.' She still thinks that they took a little more than their share but, as she said, 'that does not matter, they are my brothers.' Inheriting both urban real estate and bank shares, she sold some of both to buy a piece of land and have her own house built. Her main concern was to secure her elder daughter's future: 'So she will have a good house in the future. I want to make sure that she is safe.'

While Khawla emphasized that her brothers had been good to her, allowing her to study abroad at a time when few women did so, she still had a difficult time convincing them to divide their father's estate so that she could take her share. By doing so she acted against the unwritten rule that a woman ought to be satisfied with what comes her way and should not actively seek her share. So, although daughters in wealthy families are often given part of their share in the estate, it is expected that they should not bring up the issue themselves. Khawla did because she had both the capacity and a pressing need to do so. As a professional woman in her forties, with her own house and income, she was not too dependent on her brothers and would not need to turn to them in times of hardship. Still, the main factor which pushed her to act was to the need to secure her daughter's future.

Single and Elderly:
Rights to Housing and Maintenance

Single, elderly women find themselves in a particular position in regard to property and inheritance. Although most of those who could afford it have left the older houses in Nablus, quite a number of these are still inhabited by elderly women only. Sometimes a woman lives there by herself, more often a mother with her daughter or two sisters live together. One of those living on her own in the old city of Nablus is Sitt Salwa, a woman in her early sixties. From an artisan family background, daughter of a small workshop owner, Sitt Salwa had started to work as a seamstress when still a young girl. Later she also took care of the infant son of one of her brothers and her responsibilities increased further when her mother fell ill. By then all her brothers had married and had moved out of the house. 'Their wives left my mother to herself,' as Sitt Salwa put it.

Sitt Salwa's position as a seamstress deteriorated when after the Israeli occupation in 1967 the independent sewing trade collapsed. But it was a personal tragedy—the death of her foster son in the civil war in Jordan in 1970—which caused her to give up sewing altogether. When a few years later her mother passed away (her father had died some years earlier), she decided to go on living by herself in the family home. Yet her brothers were unhappy with the situation, fearing people's censure of their perceived unwillingness to care for their sister. She therefore went to live in her eldest brother's household for some time but, as she pointed out, 'his wife could not bear it.' Sitt Salwa felt that she was not treated well and had little privacy. After a quarrel she returned to the old family home, which she much preferred. Although her brothers remained angry with her for some time and refused to pay her maintenance, in the end everyone accepted the situation and the relationship with her brothers was mended. She never considered claiming her inheritance share, but received her mother's two gold bracelets.

Sitt Salwa's claim to the family home indicates the way in which inheritance practices relating to elderly single women are structurally different from those relating to married women. Brothers are legally obliged to provide for a single woman without means of her own and in a sense a brother's contributions to his sister's maintenance are hard to distinguish from a gradual pay-off of her inheritance share. If tensions arise, they tend to be expressed in terms of maintenance rather than in terms of inheritance. Elderly single women, however, usually hold strong usufruct rights to the paternal home. Especially when it became increasingly common for married sons to move soon after marriage into a house of their own, the most convenient solution for everyone was for an elderly unmarried daughter to remain in her father's house. Although emotional ties between a sister and her brother can be very close, and in the early years of his marriage a sister may, indeed, have more say in her brother's household than his wife, this tends to change through time, when her sister-in-law has grown children. Many times I heard older women warn girls reluctant to marry that they would end up living in their brother's house as a servant to his wife. So, while an elderly single woman usually does not demand her share in the estate, her claim on the family home is very strong and is often of central importance to her.

A Special Relationship:
Women, their Mothers and Gold

In the Jabal Nablus region women generally stand a better chance of receiving gold than of inheriting their share in landed property. A single village woman in her mid-twenties and employed as a teacher in Nablus, pointed out to me that she was quite willing to renounce her rights in the land to her brothers, because 'you never know when you will need them,' but that she would take her mother's gold. Actually, she was expecting her mother to sell some of her gold in the near future and give her the money, so she would be able to buy herself a small second-hand car and go home more regularly.

Yet it is not so much the nature of the property that is at stake, but the relation between testator and heir. Gold is, after all, mostly inherited from mothers. Because of the strong emotional bonds between a mother and daughter it is rather common for a woman to support her daughter through a donation of some of her gold during her lifetime. It is true that in poorer households women's gold may be the main disposable property available and as such it cannot always be spared for daughters. However, both in Nablus and in the rural areas, a mother often gives gold to a daughter she feels particularly responsible for and close to, for example a daughter who postponed her own marriage to take care of her ageing mother. Even if she does not do so in her lifetime, such as in the case of Sitt Salwa, this close mother-daughter tie gives women a particular claim on their mother's estate, which often consists of gold. In that sense it seems more difficult to disinherit women from gold than from any other type of property.

Claiming Property Rights:
An Indication of Distress

If married women in small property owning households do claim their share in the estate, this is often an indication of a highly problematic situation. In some cases it may well be the husband pressing his wife to claim her share, rather than she acting on her own initiative. In fact, she may do so against her own wishes. The following tale was told about one of the few women in al-Balad who had demanded her share:

This woman's husband wanted her to take the land because he had got into a fight with one of her brothers. Pressured by him, she felt forced to do so, and it destroyed her life. Her brothers had always been good to her, and they continued to present many gifts to their other sister, who had not claimed her share. But in her case, after her brothers had given her the value of the land in cash, they cut off their relations with her. This affected her so much that she fell ill and never fully recovered. Her husband did not really take care of her; he spent her money, and in the end left her to herself.

While women 'taking property from their brothers' are much censured, it is socially condoned for a daughter to claim her share under particular circumstances. If her brothers do not treat her well, neglect her and do not provide for her, a daughter who claims her rights is not condemned. Still, even under circumstances of this kind, very few women take such a step. On the other hand, for brotherless daughters, their position with respect to their fathers' estate is very different (see also Granqvist 1931: 76ff; Rosenfeld 1960: 67). In Jabal Nablus, it is socially acceptable for such daughters to claim their shares and they quite regularly try to do so. Yet, their attempts are not often successful. This is evident from the inheritance story of Umm Abdulrahim, a poor widow, working as a cleaner in a Nablus hospital.

Umm Abdulrahim's father, who had been a small landowner in the village of N, passed away when she was still an infant. As her mother remarried soon afterwards, the two small daughters were taken in by their father's brother in N. When Umm Abdulrahim was about twelve, she was married off to a man from the Majdal, in the coastal region of Palestine. A few years later, during the fighting in 1947/48 they had to flee the Majdal and came to N. By then her father's brother had taken her father's land. 'He did not want to give us any,' Umm Abdulrahim stressed, 'we had nothing. He only let us live in the old house.' Still very young and with a refugee husband, she felt in no position to challenge her paternal uncle. Recalling those days Umm Abdulrahim emphasized how difficult the situation had been. 'My husband went everywhere to find work. For a short time we lived in the Jordan Valley working as sharecroppers, then he worked for two years in Kuwait, and after that we lived for a while with our three children on the East Bank where he worked as a stonecutter.' When her husband was no longer able to do that work and they returned to N, Umm Abdulrahim and her sister finally attempted to get their share of their father's land. 'This was twenty years after he had died,' she said. 'At first, my father's brother refused adamantly. Through the mediation of others we tried to convince him and in the end, after lots of problems, the two of us together received one-quarter of our father's land, although we were entitled to more.'

Cases such as this one are fairly common. If brotherless daughters receive a share in their father's estate, it is often considerably less than what they are legally entitled to. Umm Abdulrahim, for instance, not only had to wait many years before she received the land, but also did not obtain the full amount.

A daughter without brothers has good reasons to claim her land. She may well assume, often quite rightly so, that her father's brothers will generally be less concerned about her welfare and less dependable in providing for her than brothers would have been. So even if her husband would profit most from the inheritance, it might still be a sensible strategy for a brotherless woman to take her share. The problematic situation of such a daughter is also socially recognized, as she is not condemned for claiming her share, while a man attempting to disinherit his late brother's daughters is often censured. Still, it is very difficult for her to gain de facto control over the property. If she is already married, her father's brother, usually many years her senior, will often ignore her claims and whether she receives anything may well depend on her husband's standing in the community. If she is still single her father's brother is not only the contending heir, but also her legal marriage guardian. To forestall further problems over the estate he may try to marry her to his own son, since in that way no land will be lost to strangers. As Granqvist noted in Artas, a daughter without brothers could inherit, but she had to marry within the lineage 'in order to prevent a stranger taking possession of the property and inheritance of the family'; indeed, a disproportionate number of brotherless girls had married their paternal cousin (ibn amm) (1931: 76; 78). Elsewhere on the West Bank this type of cousin marriage is also one of the most common forms of forced marriages, both for women and men. A man may have to marry a woman many years his senior simply to hold on to the land, which in turn may later induce him to take a second wife.

Widows, Sons and Agricultural Production

Umm Rubhi was widowed in 1967 when Israeli soldiers shot her husband at the river Jordan as he was trying to return from his work in Kuwait to his family on the West Bank. Twenty-seven years old at the time, with a nine-year-old son and three younger daughters, there was little doubt that she would stay with her children in her husband's home. It is true that during her husband's lifetime her relations with her mother-in-law had occasionally been tense yet, as she pointed out, there were strong family ties between them; she and her husband were from the same lineage and her brother had also married her husband's sister. And she herself had worked hard to get things her way. Through lending out some of her own money for the use of land and cultivating it herself, she had helped her husband to save in order to build a separate house next to his father's. When she was widowed no one suggested she ought to leave her husband's house. Her father-in-law had sufficient land and her son would inherit his father's share. In the meantime, she continued cultivating the land and her in-laws provided for the household. To decrease her dependence on them further she started working as a seamstress, also receiving support from one of her brothers in Kuwait, who was well-off and sent her many gifts.

For widows, even more than in the case of daughters, it is social relations rather than access to property that really count. A widow is usually more concerned about being able to keep her children than about realizing her property rights in her husband's estate. When households were still mainly dependent on agriculture for a livelihood the importance of women's labour was recognized and children were seen as an asset. If a rural widow had to give up her children it was because her kin wanted her to return home; in particular if she was young, they may have feared for her reputation and wanted her to remarry. Unless she married her husband's brother, her in-laws would not allow her to keep her children and, legally, she would be obliged to give them up.

In the case of Umm Rubhi there was no discussion about remarriage, as there were multiple and close ties of kinship between her and her in-laws, her husband had already started to build a separate house and, most importantly, she was not very young and had a son, the heir to her husband's property. In such cases, unless a husband had children by another wife, his estate would often not be divided for a long time, and even if the widow had renounced her share in her sons' favour, she would still have a relatively independent position through de facto control of their land. In households dependent on agriculture a widow can do a large part of the work herself, and for specifically male tasks solicit the help of male relatives or in-laws. While in practice this may well mean that she would be amongst the last to receive help, she may still have more autonomy than in her husband's lifetime. Once her sons are grown up, they are not only legally obliged to provide for her, but also the ties between a mother and her sons are usually emotionally and morally very strong. Under such circumstances it is uncommon for her own kin to ask her to return, and if they do so, it is not very likely that she will respond to them.

The position of a younger widow with daughters only, on the other hand, is very different and highly problematic, a situation fraught with tensions and an unpredictable outcome. While the widow herself would often prefer to stay with and care for her daughters, her future is insecure, as her daughters are to marry and will then usually not be able to provide and care for her. Her late husband's brothers are not obliged to maintain her and might well cheat her and her daughters out of their rights to the estate. Her own relatives may urge her to return home, but have no obligations towards her daughters and may pressure her into re-marriage. Emotionally this is an extremely taxing situation both for her and her daughters. It is quite evident that women without sons fear such a future from the cases in which a woman actually encourages her husband to marry another wife in order to have sons because then her husband's brothers no longer hold a claim to the property and her daughters have half-brothers to protect them.

The Burden of Providing

Even sons, however, do not always guarantee that a widow can stay with her children, as is illustrated in the case of Nuzha. From a lower-middle-class urban family, Nuzha was widowed in 1983, when she was twenty-six and mother of four small sons. She had got along well with her husband, a small shopkeeper, fifteen years her senior, but not with her (widowed) mother-in-law, with whom they were living. When her husband suddenly died, the situation escalated rapidly. Although Nuzha had four sons, her in-laws told her that she had no rights as she was still young and would probably remarry, in which case the estate would go to her new husband, as they phrased it. Although she stressed her commitment to her children by renouncing her inheritance rights for their sake, this did not help. Her in-laws refused to support her and wanted her to return to her father's house. The latter, in turn, got annoyed, told her to come home, but to leave the children behind; he was prepared to provide for her, but was under no obligation to take care of the children. To avoid this, Nuzha first tried to run her husband's store in the market area, but without the support of her own male kin or in-laws, this did not work out. Then she returned to her father's house, who finally, after she had threatened to kill herself, let her have the children stay with her. Nevertheless, because he did not allow them anything, he made their lives miserable and in the end Nuzha remarried.

Even if the case of Nuzha, a mother of four sons more or less forced to remarry, is rather exceptional, it highlights the problems an urban widow may have to confront. Because of the gender division of labour, an urban widow's economic situation often deteriorates considerably and she might well be worse off than her rural 'propertied' counterpart. In the urban cash economy, a widow is often unable to take over her husband's work, be it that of an artisan or in trade, even partially. At the same time, except for those professionally employed, very little alternative employment is available to women that is remunerative enough to provide for a household. Hence the loss of a husband means quite literally the loss of a provider and may make her dependent on charity and gifts. With both the widow and the children seen as an economic burden, all involved limit themselves to what they are obliged to provide, with her in-laws refusing to maintain the widow and her own father unwilling to spend money on her children. Under such circumstances, it is difficult for her to hold out until her sons are grown up and able to provide for the household.

While previously rural widows, at least those who managed to stay with their children, seem to have had a less dependent position, socio-economic change has also affected them. For a 'propertied' widow with sons the main question is not so much whether she receives her legal entitlement, but rather how she can deal with the property concerned. When production in the rural areas was still mainly directed towards subsistence this was easier for rural than for urban women, as the gender division of labour was less strict in the villages and more consumption goods were home-produced. Gradually, however, it has become virtually impossible to depend on dry-farming agriculture for a living and the rural population has also become more dependent on migrant wage labour. As a result the position of rural widows has weakened considerably and has become more similar to that of urban widows. For rural women, too, losing a husband has also come to mean losing a provider, with widowhood synonymous with impoverishment.

The Complexities of Power and Property

In this chapter I have proposed a shift in focus from the nature of the property inherited to the position of the women involved. The material presented here indicates that in order to understand women's inheritance strategies it is important to focus on a complex web of gendered social relations: position with respect to kin, in terms of social stratification, marital status and division of labour. The presence or absence of contending heirs is central to whether women refrain from claiming their inheritance share or not. It is brotherless daughters (and their widowed mothers) who show most interest in claiming their share. The daughters of wealthy households are the ones who stand the best chance of inheriting some of their father's property, while single, elderly women hold on to usufruct rights in their father's house.

Another related point raised in the introduction concerns the assumed relationship between property and power. Historians, in particular, who by virtue of their sources have more information about property than about the women concerned or about their motives, often consider property ownership as an indication of a relatively autonomous position and as an embodiment of power. The material presented here points to the multiple meanings of inheriting property and argues for a modification of the assumed positive relation between power and property.

Claiming property rights does not necessarily denote power. Some women receive part of their share automatically because they are from an urban, wealthy family background and men can raise their own status by giving to their sisters, yet the latter are not supposed to enquire about their rights. In such cases women's access to property is an expression of their class position. Others inherit because their husbands put great pressure on them to claim their share. Far from being an expression of power, such female heirs are not only likely to lose kin support, but to end up in a weaker position *vis-à-vis* their husband and his kin. On the other hand, there are also women who attempt to claim their share because they find themselves in a particularly vulnerable position, such as daughters who do not have brothers.

In a similar vein, while claiming one's property rights is not always an indication of power, neither does refraining from claiming one's share necessarily mean giving up all rights to it. Daughters may adopt the latter strategy as they identify emotionally with their kin, and as such share in their prosperity. Being ultimately dependent on them for their socio-economic security, it actually may make sense for women to do so in order to highlight their kin's obligations towards them. In historical perspective not claiming one's inheritance rights can, in fact, be seen as an optimizing strategy. From the 1950s onwards, with the rapid increase in migrant male wage-labour and the marginalization of agriculture, men's responsibilities as providers and women's dependence as consumers has been reinforced. With a greater emphasis on conjugality rather than kinship, women are increasingly defined as wives, rather than as daughters and sisters. Admittedly, women argue that they do not claim their inheritance share as their brothers have to provide for their own households, yet they also point out that they prefer to do so since it enables them to still call upon the support of their kin *vis-à-vis* their husbands. If women had really opted for conjugality they would have taken their share in their father's estate and handed it over to their husbands whose marital power would be enhanced. In this sense holding on to the strategy of refraining from claiming one's inheritance may be seen as the best option available in a delicate balancing act where women try to optimize the room for manoeuvre which exists in a particular gender system. It does, however, leave women dependent on their male kin, who may in the end not be very dependable, and increasingly less so with changing forms of livelihood which encourage greater reliance on marital ties. Shifting the focus from property as a material resource to property as a gendered social relation thus helps to gain insight into the complexities of the relations between property, power and gender.

Notes

This research has been supported by the Foundation for Social and Cultural Sciences, which is subsidized by the Netherlands Organization for Scientific Research (NWO). A more elaborate version of this chapter can be found in *Women, Property and Islam: Palestinian experiences, 1920–1990* (forthcoming, Cambridge University Press).

References

Gerber, H. (1980) 'Social and economic position of women in an Ottoman city, Bursa', *International Journal of Middle East Studies*, 12: 231–44.

Granqvist, H. (1931) *Marriage Conditions in a Palestinian Village, I*, Akademische Buchhandlung.

—— (1935) *Marriage Conditions in a Palestinian Village, II*, Helsingfors: Helsingfors, Akademische Buchhandlung.

Jennings, R. (1975) 'Women in early 17th century Ottoman judicial records—the Shari'a court of Anatolian Kayseri', *Journal of the Economic and Social History of the Orient*, 18: 53–114.

Layish, A. (1975) *Women and Islamic Law in a non-Muslim State*, New York: Wiley.

Marcus, A. (1983) 'Men, women and property: dealers in real estate in 18th century Aleppo', *Journal of the Economic and Social History of the Orient*, 26: 137–63.

Pastner, C. (1980) 'Access to property and the status of women in Islam', in J. Smith (ed.), *Women in Contemporary Muslim Societies*, Lewisbury: Bucknell University Press, pp. 146–86.

Peters, E. (1978) 'The status of women in four Middle Eastern communities' in L. Beck and N. Keddie (eds), *Women in the Muslim World*, Cambridge Mass.: Harvard University Press, pp. 311–51.

Rosenfeld, H. (1960) 'On the determinants of the status of Arab village women', *Man* 40: 66–74.

Whitehead, A. (1984) 'Men and women, kinship and property: some general issues' in R. Hirshon (ed.), *Women and Property, Women as Property*, London and Canberra: Croom Helm, pp. 176–93.

5

Adam and Adama, 'Ird and Ard: En-gendering Political Conflict and Identity in Early Jewish and Palestinian Nationalisms

Sheila Hannah Katz

> It ought to be possible for historians…to 'make visible the assign-
> ment of subject-positions' [Gayatri Spivak] not in the sense of
> capturing the reality of objects seen, but of trying to understand the
> operations of the complex and changing discursive process by which
> identities are ascribed, resisted, or embraced, and which processes
> themselves are unremarked and indeed achieve their effect because
> they are unnoticed.[1]

In turn-of-the-century Palestine, there occurred a re-imagination
of identities. Older loyalties to village, religion and empire both
contended and colluded with a growing secular nationalism.[2] As
the Ottoman Empire collapsed, Palestinians who had been law-
abiding subjects were compelled to shift allegiances. Jews in
Europe, who had long been legally released from high-walled
ghettos, grappled with broken promises and violent threats.[3]

I will argue in this chapter that gender issues were central to
the formation of nationalist responses to these challenges. The
changing roles of women and men in Jewish and Arab society
played an important, though hidden, role in the formation of
national identities and new national identities, in turn, influenced
evolving gender roles. Changing images of women, men and community contributed to shaping specific power relations between
and among Jews and Arabs.

This chapter examines different ways in which gendered processes were central to the formation of two competing nationalisms
in Palestine before 1950. It draws upon materials published inside
and outside Palestine which reflected and directed efforts by Jews
and Arabs to redefine 'peoplehood' before 1950.[4] Kimmerling and
Migdal refer to these published writings as 'furnishing a shared

aesthetic and intellectual material...of the new Palestinism—a cultural glue.'[5] Political tracts,[6] revisionist histories,[7] newspaper and magazine articles,[8] biographies,[9] autobiographies,[10] memoirs,[11] novels,[12] poetry,[13] and films,[14] gave expression to these nascent nationalisms.

These writings were not limited to Arabs and Jews who lived in Palestine. Egyptians, Lebanese, Syrians and many others who never went there also participated in the imagining of a new national community and in discussing the nature of gender relations within it. Jews from the diaspora, who visited or merely fantasized about Palestine, also contributed to constructions of manhood, womanhood and peoplehood there.

A few of the sources self-consciously and even vociferously addressed 'the woman question', while most others offered implicit, unspoken assumptions about the place of gender in nationalism.[15] Almost all shared the conscious sense that women and gender issues were irrelevant, or at best marginal, to the national project. Yet taken in their entirety, these writings expose the centrality of women and gender in the construction of political identities.

Two scholarly breakthroughs in the 1980s provided a theoretical and methodological framework for the interrogation of gender-nation relations. In 1983, Benedict Anderson, in *Imagined Communities*, talked about nationalism as a set of cultural constructions.[16] In 1988, Joan Wallach Scott elaborated on the significance of reading for silences about women in historical texts, and the importance of constructions of gender for an understanding of power in high politics. In *Gender and the Politics of History*, Scott asserted that 'those absent from official accounts partook nonetheless in the making of history; those who are silent speak eloquently about the meaning of power and uses of political authority.'[17]

Reading nationalist texts is a lesson in the power of silence. Nowhere do women and issues of gender seem more remote than in the narratives of political history, where women are absent and men ubiquitous. Volumes of Palestinian and Israeli analyses hardly yield a word about national actors as gendered beings and generate an overwhelming impression that gender is irrelevant to politics. Yet it is upon this seeming irrelevance that particular political arrangements depend which bolster hierarchies of difference based on gender, class, race and ethnicity.

National narratives are, in fact, gendered texts at a number of different levels: (1) in the centrality of notions of manhood and masculinity to nationalism, (2) in the feminization of the land as the central symbol of survival, (3) in the ways nationalists imagined women, (4) in the ways modernization co-opted gender to shape nationalism, and (5) in the ways women colluded with or contested these constructions.

Nationalism and Manhood

While women and men both actively participated in what they understood to be a movement for liberation, it was men as leaders and propagandists who defined both problems and solutions in ways that linked nationalism to the achievement of manhood.

The Arab Palestinian martyr Abd al-Rahim Mahmud proclaimed in a poem: 'I will guard my land with my sword so that all will know that I am a man!'[18] Benjamin, a fictional Jewish teenage Holocaust survivor, proclaimed in a film that 'God needed earth to make a man, and I need earth to become a man!'[19] The proof or achievement of manhood was thus a persistent subtext of nationalist narratives. The bronzed, muscular farmer/soldier 'New Man' was the Zionist alternative to his stooped, intellectual and victimized diaspora predecessor. Jews associated the *galut* with characteristics deemed negatively feminine such as being passive or vulnerable victims. In a sense men felt relegated to being symbolic women, that is, subject to degradation and abuse by other men of dominant cultures.

The 'New Man' of Zionism was supposed to throw off the powerlessness of two thousand years. As architect of this myth, Berdichevsky interpreted exile as both an external and internal condition. Deep within the soul, beneath the dust of Rabbinic Judaism, there lay a primordial element which needed to be set free.[20] This meant taking a stand to physically defend oneself as well as one's women and children.[21]

The Palestinian Arab patriarch, whether peasant or poet, was supposed to defend his *ard* and his *'ird*, his land and his women's sexual integrity. As an antidote to centuries of foreign rule, Palestinian men expressed rage at dispossession which could result in exile. At the very point in history when they could begin to imagine power residing in the hands of a new class of Palestinian men, they perceived betrayal and abandonment by other men be they Jewish, British, Arab or, most bitterly, Palestinian. Possession and defence of the land and women were at the centre not only of emerging national consciousness but of individual men's self-respect. As Fawaz Turki asserted, 'to Palestinians, no phrase is more familiar—perhaps one should call it a metaphrase—than *ardi-'irdi.*' Translated literally it means 'my land is my womenfolk.' As understood by Palestinians, the phrase reads, 'my land is my nobility...my being what I am.'[22]

The prominent Palestinian writer, Muhammad Izzat Darwazah, wrote the novel *al-Malak wa'l-simsar* (The Angel and the Land Broker) representing a typical Palestinian Arab family of the mid-1920s. The protagonist was an illiterate but nevertheless dignified head of household. A Jewish land broker, representing Zionists' deceptions and the temptations of modernity, enticed the father to go to the city to enjoy himself. There the man spent all his money and was forced to mortgage his house to the broker for an amount in excess of its value. He then spent all this money in the city and was ultimately shamed into deserting his family, becoming a beggar, finally ending up in an insane asylum.[23] Jews and the modern development they hastened were depicted as responsible for the moral and material downfall of innocent Arab men.

The importance of the defence of land and the political conditions which made this goal ultimately impossible to achieve fostered a culture of martyrdom. Abd al-Rahim Mahmud, poet and martyr, reasoned that real men had two choices: to live with honour or to die fighting for it.[24] Ibrahim Tuqan, the prominent Palestinian poet from Nablus wrote *al-Shahid* (The Martyr), in which he described the full honour accorded a man who was strong and unafraid of danger, pain or death. Tuqan wrote that even if no one knew about the way he died, nobody cried at his death, or no one knew the location of his grave, the matter of his body was unimportant because his name would be everywhere: 'O how joyous was his face when he was passing to death; singing to the whole world: could I but sacrifice myself for God and my country.'[25]

Feminization of the Land

Beyond preoccupations with the preservation or recuperation of manhood, the symbols of the nation were saturated with gendered meaning. Land became a central symbol of both national and personal redemption. Jewish men called themselves 'Zionists' because the rebirth of their peoplehood and manhood depended on their claim to *Eretz Tzion*, the Land of Zion. Arab men began to think of themselves as 'Filastini' to distinguish themselves from other Arabs who were not directly attached to the land of Palestine and its distinctive colonial conundrum. Imagining Zion or Palestine as female turned its defenders into real men.

Outside the Land of Zion, Zionists referred to the Jewish people not merely as female, but as the quintessential downtrodden girl. Pinsker claimed: 'He [the Jew] is treated as a Cinderella; in the most favorable cases he is regarded as an adopted child whose rights may be questioned, never is he considered a legitimate child of the fatherland.'[26] But in Palestine these weak, feminized people were transformed into powerful males wooing a female land. The desire of men to possess this land made them imbue it with feminine characteristics. Sometimes the land was depicted as the lover to be conquered and fertilized; at other times it became the mother giving birth to a new 'masculine' people.

In 1909, on the commune of Bittania, for example, the charismatic leader, Meir Yaari, equated the land with both a bride and a fertile mother. This transformed the Jewish people into both sons and the

> ...bridegroom who abandons himself in his bride's bosom...thus we abandon ourselves to the motherly womb of sanctifying earth...In this last hour before our wedding night, we bring as holy sacrifice to you, earth of our fulfilment, these our very lives, our daily lives in the land of Israel; our parents, children, brothers, our poverty and wealth.[27]

A.D. Gordon articulated an ideology of redemption through physical labour on the land. He portrayed Jewish men willing to leave materially comfortable lives in the *galut* for the physical hardships of life in Palestine comparing Jews to a man burning for his lover: 'The lover prefers a dry morsel of bread in a poor cottage in the company of his beloved to a life of luxury without her. Whoever separates him from his beloved deprives him of life.'[28]

With a Hebrew play on words, Buber elaborated on the marriage analogy. In Hebrew, *adam* is the name for the first male human in the Bible. *Ben adama*, son of Adam, becomes 'human' or 'man'. *Adama*, the female form of the word, is not the word for woman, but the word for 'land'. So, Buber articulated his belief in 'the great marriage between *adam* and *adama*'.[29]

Feminizing and eroticizing the land as passive object of men's active love and sacrifice transformed the Palestinian people into men. The poet Iskandar al-Khuri al-Baytjali, for example, lamented over Palestine as an emaciated female weakened by foreign rule. The possession and care of this land by Palestinian men would infuse her with strength and health:

> Strength has spread through her body and penetrated deeply into her bosom.
> She was petrified after being weak and thin.
> This is Palestine, who until recently was at a loss and humiliated by the Turks.
> She has become languid, while she was bright at the time of the Arabs.[30]

In the 1930s, Ajaj Nuwiyhid portrayed Palestine as the bride of Arab men, a bride which had to be won at the highest cost, with the blood of the groom. Dying for the beloved proved men's unquestionable love:

> We have asked to become engaged to a girl
> Her bride price is very expensive
> But she deserves it
> Here is our answer:
> We will fight for the sake of your eyes.
> Death is our aim
> and we have many men.[31]

Men's love for the land was sometimes opposed to the love of actual women. The words under the Rashadiyya school club map of Palestine read: 'Palestine, the blessed land…best land of all! Do not despair. You are the only love we have.'[32] Real women were left behind, widowed or turned into reasons for fighting.

Imagined Women

If nationalists feminized the central symbol of their desire, the land, and derided feminine traits as characterizing their worst perceptions of themselves, how then did they imagine women?

We return to the young hero, Benjamin, conscious of needing land to become a man, but totally unaware of his need for a woman to help him get there.[33] It is Miriam's love for Benjamin which enables him to shed an impenetrable shell acquired from living half a young life in death camps. As another Holocaust orphan at this camp in Palestine, Miriam offers an intelligent love, which breaks down Benjamin's resistance to grasping the hoe and marching out of isolation to work with other barefooted young men on a land representing new possibilities of manhood. As for Miriam, what she needs most to become a woman is a man.

Basically, women were imagined as good or bad according to how much they helped or hindered men in achieving their goals. Herzl praised women when their 'enthusiasm lent wings to the men's courage.'[34] Arab men paid tribute to wives for sacrificing their own money and labour to the cause of the homeland. In the midst of a detailed account of Palestinian military battles, Arif al-Arif interrupted his narrative to praise the wife of the hero, Abd al-Qadir. Remaining nameless in the text, the wife was praised for helping fighters by cooking for them and washing their clothes, thereby elevating wifely chores to national service.[35]

Motherhood, however, was presented as the highest form of national service. Muhammad Bindari wrote:

> A woman must first prove her success inside the house by raising her children to love their country. She must strengthen their national feeling and nurse them with the milk of nationalism.[36]

As 'patriotic' wombs, it was not enough for women merely to marry and have children. They also played a central role as boundary markers of national identities. One study of Palestine was critical of the dearth of intermarriage across class lines during the Mandate period, resulting from townspeople's disdain for peasants, as something that weakened national bonds.[37] For Jews, class was also an issue but not one as threatening as inter-faith marriages. In Europe, intermarriage with non-Jews was tantamount to cultural genocide. In the national context of Palestine it was treason because it blurred distinctions between the categories of Jew and Arab.[38]

'Nationalization' of sexuality meant that women were restricted to sexual relations with 'their own kind'. Yet among Jews in Palestine, it also meant that intermarriage between European and Palestinian or Arab Jews was approved as promoting progress. A biographer of Golda Meir, towards the end of a long account of her political accomplishments, capped her achievements with a description of her grandchildren:

> Youth filled the room...blond, blue-eyed Sabras of European and American origin; dusky Yemenites whose presence testified to the mingling of East and West in the authentic melting pot of Israel...Golda's

own grandchildren highlighted the contrasts: the blond, blue-eyed babies of Menachem and the dark beauty of the children of Sarale.[39]

Hierarchies of power and prestige are absent from this cheerful description which levels difference to attractive physical traits. The blending of races, or the protection of distinctions between them, was lauded or condemned depending on evolving political identities. Meir's granddaughter, Naomi, born of an Ashkenazi mother and Palestinian Jewish father, represented the union of what was hoped to be the best of Western and Eastern Jewry. Naomi was considered to have an unselfconscious 'authenticity' of national identity, for she was 'at last free of the idea of Zion; she was part of its hills, its sun, and sand.'[40]

While men were expected to give their lives for the new nation, women were to give birth to new fighters, sacrifice sons and husbands for the cause and bear their grief as a badge of honour. When one Jewish mother in South Africa received news that her young son had died fighting the British in Palestine,

> her first reaction to the news of his death was to say quietly that if her son had to die in war, she was glad he had not given up his precious young life for others, but had died fighting for his own people...A year later her broken heart gave up its struggle with sorrow and quietly ceased beating.[41]

Yet not all women married and conceived children. Apparently there was a substantial enough number of women who for one reason or another did not marry for Herzl, in his novel about a utopian Jewish society, to plan an entire branch of government to be run by them.[42] In *Altneuland*, Herzl envisioned a society in which women who were cast off as 'old maids' in Europe would not have to live what were assumed to be 'wasteful' lives. He imagined single women taking charge of the 'philanthropic' or 'welfare' arm of the state. They would provide care for the sick, poor, orphaned and needy, running hospitals, orphanages, vacation camps and public kitchens, becoming mothers of the nation where they had failed to become mothers of families.

Women and Modernization

The discourse of modernization underpinned many of the constructions of gender and nation. Whether waxing eloquent on the future of 'barren wastelands' or in volatile debates about women's rights, nationalists, as self-appointed modernizers, imagined women as both the vehicles and the objects of civilization. They were a measure of the advancement or backwardness of a culture. Muhammad Bahim, for example, asserted that:

> The development of women is more important for measuring the development of a country than its construction of sky-high buildings and wide boulevards.[43]

Kumari Jayawardena noted in her analysis of women's roles in nationalist movements throughout the Third World that 'the status of women in society was the popular barometer of "civilization".'[44] Education, freedom of movement and monogamy became hallmarks of 'civilized' modernity. The 'New Man' needed a 'New Woman' to be presentable in colonialist circles, rather than secluded, veiled or illiterate. Modernization would tolerate no more bound feet or bound minds. British, Arab and Zionist leaders all gave their attention to the process of 'modernizing' women as a measure of the legitimacy of their power in Palestine.

The primary focus of much of this attention was on education for girls. Girls' education was a basic element of both colonialist and nationalist policy. British interest in female education remained fraught with contradictions. On the one hand, it was to their advantage to appear to encourage girls' schooling. The ideals of the Mandate dictated that British presence should promote a new level of civilization with education as its primary vehicle. British policy identified girls' instruction as one of its three most important goals, along with agricultural and technical education. The post of Education Inspectorate was thus immediately created and filled with Englishwomen, who opened a teacher training college for women.[45]

When girls were actually permitted to attend school, the policy was to teach them 'to understand the value of a good home where cleanliness, sanitation, and above all care of children are to be regarded as the aim of every woman.'[46] Within the framework of modernization, this was labelled the study of 'domestic science'.[47] Yet British policies to maintain the status quo, especially in the villages, inevitably impeded change for women. The administrators never failed, however, to blame this failure on 'Islam'.

Arab educators, for their part, attributed the shortcomings of the system, not to Islam, but to British policies. A.L. Tibawi, for example, pointed out that Islam did not oppose girls' education but that British planning and budgeting bolstered a defective and inadequate system. Drawing upon a combination of religious scriptures and social sciences, Tibawi argued for educational reform that would modernize and strengthen his community. He pointed out that the Prophet declared 'the quest for learning is a sacred duty of every Muslim, male and female.' He also argued that social prejudice and inequality between men and women was a result of low education levels for men, so that increasing the levels of men's education would lead to an improvement for women.[48]

Cooking, childbirth and child care, health and hygiene, sewing and embroidery which had until then been learned within the family became legitimate material for school curricula. But the process of attending school was more radical than curriculum content. Removing girls from their homes, bringing them together with others outside their extended family network, and teaching them to read dramatically changed women's lives on a variety of levels. These changes for women came to symbolize progress for modernizing nationalists.

Others, however, argued that progress could only come through resisting changes for women in order to preserve imagined values of the past. Women were seen as the repository of a way of life or guardians of threatened 'authentic' values that offered viable alternatives to Western secular ones. Lamya Baha al-Din of Gaza voiced this position in a letter published on the pages of the Jerusalem daily, al-Difa, saying that:

> these women will forget their roles in the homes and seek modernization. A good woman must not covet modernization but be proud of the chains that the community puts on her. She must be satisfied with her traditions without complaining.[49]

In the Yishuv, the terms of discourse were different, although similarly determined by concerns about progress. Education was made compulsory for all girls and boys. Funding from abroad enabled the Jewish settlers to overcome the limits set on education by the British administration, and organizations placed top priority on the creation of educational opportunities for all Jewish children. The budget for Hebrew language schools alone exceeded the budget of British government schools for Arabs.[50]

Jewish nationalists were acutely aware of the potency of education in furthering national goals. Noah Nardi complained that Arab education was becoming a 'negative' force in Palestine for 'the Arab school system maintained by the government has constantly inculcated in Arab children a hostile attitude to Jewish aspirations in Palestine.'[51] Yet when education served the interests of Jewish national feeling, Nardi naturally interpreted its effects as 'constructive'.

Nationalist objectives for Jewish education in Palestine reflected widespread assumptions about the importance of public education for the production of a loyal citizenry. Nardi wrote:

> The child must be imbued with a love for Palestine and a desire to live in it and be satisfied with whatever it can offer him...He must acquire a strong nationalist consciousness and loyalty...He must learn to understand and co-operate with his Arab neighbors.[52]

For the first time in Jewish history girls received up to secondary level education in unprecedented numbers. But their education did not stop there. They also participated in after-school youth activities. Hanoar Haoved (the Organization of Working Youth) was an organ of the Histadrut which sought to improve working conditions for young people through the creation of evening schools, clubs and study groups. During World War II girls who attended secondary schools also had to do a year of national service harvesting crops on farms. They also attended schools for agricultural, vocational and teacher training.

These opportunities, however, did not reach all Jewish girls. Those girls who emigrated from Arab countries had a more difficult time realizing them. They were forced to work unlimited hours, receive the lowest pay, and take apprenticeships without any opportunity for mastery. Illiteracy and early marriages persisted during these years. Many girls did not go to work or school but performed traditional domestic duties in their own homes.[53]

Education for girls was not the only road to 'modernization'. Proof of women's equality to men in other fields also served as a yardstick for progressiveness. Most importantly, progressiveness was seen as a measure of the legitimacy of one's claim to Palestine. In Jewish national texts, often the only time women were mentioned was in attempts to describe how progressive Jewish Palestinian society was by lauding women's equal status. The British Zionist, Norman Bentwich, observed in the 1920s that 'the equal part of men and women in all vocations and professions is one of the outstanding features of Jewish social life in Palestine.'[54] This statement was made at a time when a few Jewish women in Palestine struggled with some remarkable successes against unremitting opposition from well-meaning comrades when they attempted to undertake non-traditional jobs.[55]

Herzl's novel, *Altneuland*, epitomized some of the ambivalence men felt about equal rights for women. The novel conveys the sense that every modern nation has the collective right to exist in part because of the individual rights it confers upon its citizens, regardless of gender or ethnicity. Here, however, is a passage that trivializes the concept of equality. One of the protagonists explains to a visitor that both Arabs and women have full rights in the New Society, but he qualifies its implications regarding his wife:

> 'Don't imagine that our women are not devoted to their homes. My wife, for instance, never goes to meetings.'

> Sarah smiled, 'But that's only because of [the baby] Fritzchen.'

> 'Yes,' continued David, 'she nursed our little boy, and so forgot a bit about her inalienable rights. She used to belong to the radical opposition. This how I met her, as an opponent. Now she opposes me only at home, as loyally as you can imagine, however.'

> [The visitor replied] 'That's a damned good way of overcoming an opposition.'[56]

Women could thus be cast as symbols of immutable or essential qualities of nationhood. The status of women could become proof of the admirable advancement or the dreaded degeneracy of Western ways. Women could be bastions of secular nationalist values or fortresses of traditionalism. They were either exemplary citizens without ever achieving full rights or subversives when they attempted to achieve those rights.

Collusion and Contestation

Despite men's limiting vision of the good 'nationalist' woman and despite the obstacles placed before them, some Palestinian Arab and Jewish women fought for the fruits of equality and even contested national boundaries. Jewish women picked up hoes, pickaxes, and attended policy-planning forums on farming, broke stones for road-building, and raised their voices in political meetings despite fierce opposition from egalitarian-minded comrades. Palestinian women as wives, sisters or daughters of the upper-class male elite founded charitable organizations which became public arenas for their leadership or wrote books, articles, poetry and letters to editors.

Some Palestinian women who entered the public arena did so because they believed that the success of their nation depended upon raising the status of women. In 1937, Matiel Mogannam wrote *The Arab Woman and the Palestine Problem* which detailed the organizational efforts by middle- and upper-class Muslim and Christian Arab women to uplift their less advantaged sisters as a way of promoting progress in their country.[57] In 1947, Salwa Sardah urged men to support women's rights in a poem in *Sawt al-mar'a al-hur* (The Free Voice of Woman) published in Aleppo.

> To those in high positions,
> To the masters of all time,
> To those who are the hope of their country during war,
> and the reason for happiness,
> To all of you, I want to ask a question and I need an answer.
> Who delivered you men and trained you to be so strong and brave as
> lions?
> Who taught you to be honest and who helped you reach high?
> This is woman,
> don't forget her goodness.
> If you forget, we are lost.
> Help her when she begs you for education and is willing to pay the
> price with her spirit and money.
> Eastern men, listen to her and give her what she asks,
> Because she brings you happiness and honour.[58]

Jewish women in Palestine became notorious for trespassing the boundaries of conventional gender roles. Recently, many scholars have debunked myths of gun-toting, sexy, female farmer/ soldiers but this does not detract from the remarkable achievements of some. Manya Shohat, for instance, initiated the idea and first attempt at collective agriculture which later evolved into the kibbutz. Women organized all-female agricultural collectives when they were excluded from or subordinated in men's settlements. They founded women's agricultural and vocational training schools and became farmers, teachers, construction workers and doctors. Yet the highly publicized gains of Jewish women in Palestine obscured the ongoing failure of that society as a whole to deal with women as equals.

Obstacles to equality and women's responses to these obstacles changed from one period to another. Some of the settlers of the first *aliya*, for example, still adhered to religious authority. So these women employed religious arguments and precedents to argue that they should take part in decision making.[59] Women of the second *aliya* who internalized the ideals of transformation of self through labour on land, were compelled to fight for the right to plant trees and clean chicken coops.[60]

Two significant features limited the gains of Jewish and Palestinian women of this period. Almost all Palestinian and Jewish women who transgressed the boundaries of gender convention did so only for the sake of their nation. This meant that as national goals were realized, women retreated into older roles. The second limitation had to do with power imbalances within and between the two peoples. Women played undeclared roles in the construction of hierarchies of difference and inequality within their communities in contradictory ways. As women became nationalists, they accepted their role in the civilizing mission. They were thus enlisted in the enforcement of divisions between women along lines of class and race, as some women dedicated themselves to help, uplift or emancipate their more 'backward' sisters.

As upper-class women assumed their roles as reformers of their people, they formed charitable organizations which made significant contributions to other women's lives. But the elitist context of modernization often imbued these efforts with a patronizing attitude that inhibited potentially powerful alliances. One Arab Christian woman, for example, complained that she had worked hard with Muslim women to 'raise them a bit' but that it was difficult to change the Muslim character.[61] A European Jewish woman watched her Jewish neighbours from Turkey and Morocco 'languish' in what appeared to her to be listless apathy at their 'appalling standards of sanitation'.[62] Each day she went to their homes to teach them modern hygiene and housekeeping but seemed oblivious to what she could learn from them.

Yet women on all sides of these lines contested divisions and occasionally crossed boundaries of class, nation and race. A Palestinian Christian woman, for example, who was hired to work on a Jewish settlement was treated and paid with respect and equality. It made such an impact on her life that one of her sons spent his lifetime attempting to implement her vision by defending Arab rights in the context of respect for Israelis.[63]

There were always significant outcomes of contacts between Arab or Arab–Jewish and European Jewish women. All colonial ventures succeeded to some extent due to indigenous women's knowledge and skills which enabled colonists to survive in a strange land. In 1907, for example, when Sejera became the first Jewish settlement to admit women, women from Kurdistan taught the European women how to sift barley.[64] In another settlement, an Arab woman taught a Jewish woman how to wash the grain that came mixed with red earth so that three layers formed separating the earth from the wild grass and the clean wheat.[65] The Jewish woman went on to become the expert in grain washing on her settlement.

Arab women taught Jewish women to make shelters out of mud, lime and straw. In one incident, an Arab woman saved Jewish lives by warning them of imminent attack. She had been selling eggs to the settlers and felt obliged to warn them even at the risk of her own life, because of kindness that settler women had shown her children.[66]

During the Arab attacks on Jews in Jaffa in 1921, the only Jews who were not massacred were those few who managed to flee or were concealed by their Arab neighbours. In one instance, because of the relationship that had evolved between neighbouring women whose children played together, the father of the Arab family withstood a beating by the attackers, telling his family that he was ready to give his own life rather than sacrifice his neighbours.[67]

As workers, Jewish women and Arab women organized and maintained strikes together against Arab and Jewish establishments.[68] As mothers, they nursed each others' children.[69] As prisoners of British jails, they helped each other survive or escape.[70] Jewish women set up organizations that recognized Arab rights to Palestine.[71] However, for the most part women defined and solidified rather than contested and dissolved boundaries, colluding in the creation of new hierarchies of power between and amongst the two peoples. Gender joined race, religion and class as a means of perpetuating conflict as well as legitimizing and transforming power arrangements that would determine who won and who lost Palestine.

Threats emanating from the 'Other' were often sexualized. The rumours of the Jewish brutality towards Palestinian women and children at Deir Yassin, precipitated a crisis for men forced to choose between defence of their women's sexual honour, *'ird*, or defence of land, *ard*. Fear of rape and murder of Jewish women by

Arab men served as a rationalization to further militarize the Yishuv. Vladimir Jabotinsky argued before the British Parliament:

> A very important factor in implementing the Mandate is looking after security…In Palestine, we were threatened with pogroms, we were telling so to the government for years and years, but they went on cutting down and cutting down on the number of troops in Palestine. We said, 'Remember that we have children and wives, legalize our self-defence!'[72]

Hatred of the enemy and necessity of self-defence was often measured by the level of perceived brutality to women. Some Jews judged the British as 'just as bad as the Germans' because an officer dragged a pregnant woman by her hair when she did not carry out their curfew order quickly enough. In another instance, after an Arab siege of a Jewish settlement, women who had taken up posts high on the top of a water tower saw themselves surrounded by Arabs without hope of reinforcements and jumped to their death rather than live through the sexual torture they feared would follow their capture.[73]

Conclusion

The foregoing illustrates some of the ways in which national identities were formed and articulated against a field of gendered meanings. Through concerns about manhood or objectifications of mother earth and earthly mothers, nationalists privileged the status of women and the development of land as means to gauge progress and the legitimacy of claims to Palestine. Women's sexuality remained a site for conflict and contestation. Discourse on gender was as important to the 'imagining' of new national communities as were, in Benedict Anderson's view, mother tongue, the capitalist press and the invention of ancient histories.[74] It served not only to establish the boundaries of national identity, but to define the 'Other' and to legitimize new forms of domination over the 'Other'.

The subordination of women and privileging of certain men in nation-building were mediated by discourses on 'real' men, imagined women, ancient heroes, barren wastelands, debates on women's rights and girls' education, motherhood and definitions of national sacrifice. Exile and dispossession, anti-Semitism and foreign colonization were ultimate dangers to all but particularly destructive to men's ability to earn livelihoods or to defend *'ird* and *ard*. In response, nationalists feminized a land imagined to redeem manhood and peoplehood in an eternal marriage of *adam* and *adama*.

The use of gender as a tool of analysis makes it possible to write an integrative history of Palestine where there have been at least two antagonistic narratives. One can interrogate these histories and subject them to similar scrutiny, exposing the operations of power within each group as well as between them. It is in these two conflicting and seemingly contradictory movements in Palestine that one gets a vivid sense of consistency regarding the ways that gender permeated politics. Nationalists seized upon gender to formulate new political identities, as women and men seized upon nationalism to construct femininities and masculinities. The study of gender as product and signifier of 'modernity' and 'nation' in these literatures provides perspective on multiple relations of power which 'en-gendered' political conflict in Palestine.

Notes

1. Joan Wallach Scott, 'Evidence of Experience', *Critical Inquiry*, 17 (1991): 793.

2. For an account of some of these changes see Muhammad Muslih, *The Origins of Palestinian Nationalism* (N.Y.: Columbia University Press, 1989).

3. For responses to these changes see Jehuda Reinharz and Paul Mendes-Flohr (eds), *The Jew in the Modern World: A documentary history* (New York: Oxford University Press, 1980).

4. Timewise, the texts range from as early as Yehuda Alkalai, 1798–1878, who wrote *Minhat Yehuda* (The Offering of Yehuda) in 1845, to as late as Asma Tubi's collection of biographies of women in *Abir wa Majd* in 1955.

5. Baruch Kimmerling and Joel Migdal, *The Palestinians: The making of a people* (New York: The Free Press, Macmillan, 1993).

6. i.e. Sa'adi Bsisu, *al-Sahyuniyyah* (Jerusalem: al-Matba'a al-Tajariyyah, 1945) or Moses Hess, *Rom und Jerusalem* (trans. Meyer Waxman, N.Y.: Bloch, 1943).

7. i.e. Arif al-Arif, *al-Nakba* (Beirut: al-Maktabah al-Asriyyah, 1947–52, or Norman Bentwich, *Palestine* (London: Ernst Benn, 1934).

8. i.e. *al-Difa* or *Majalat al-mar'a*.

9. Many biographies were written after 1948 but contained salient references to an earlier period such as Taysir Jbara, *Palestinian Leader Hajj Amin al-Husayni: Mufti of Jerusalem* (Princeton: The Kingston Press, 1985).

Others were contemporary such as Marvin Lowenthal, *Henrietta Szold: Life and letters* (New York: Viking Press, 1942).

10. Like biographies, autobiographies were often written later but dealt substantively with the pre-1948 period as did Atallah Mansour, *Waiting for the Dawn* (London: Secker and Warburg, 1975) or Henia Fekelman, *Ha'yai Po'elet be-Aretz* (Tel Aviv, 1938).

11. i.e. Rachel Katznelson-Shazar (ed.) *Divre Poalot* (The Plough Woman: memoirs of the pioneer women of Palestine) (New York: Nicholas L. Brown, 1932; revised edition, Herzl Press, 1975).

12. i.e. Muhammad Darwazah, *al-Malak wa'l-simsar* (Nablus, 1934) or Theodor Herzl, *Altneuland* (1902, trans. Lotte Levinson, New York: Herzl Press, 1960).

13. i.e. Rachel Blaustein or Abu Salma.

14. i.e. *Sabra*, directed by Alexander Ford, produced by Tzabar 1933.

15. There were books that addressed 'the woman question' such as Mustafa Sabri, *Qawli fi al-mar'a* (My Opinion about Women) (Cairo: al-Matba'a al-Salfiyah, 1935) and those which tied the issue of women's status to larger problems in Palestine such as Halifah Ajlal, *al-Mar'a wa qadiyyat Filastin* (Woman and the Palestinian Case) (Cairo: al-Matba'a al-Arabiyya al-Haditha, n.d.) More common, however, were texts which focused on something else such as nationalism or autobiography but made implicit statements on gender such as David Ben-Gurion's *Be-Maarachah* (Tel Aviv, 1948).

16. Benedict Anderson, *Imagined Communities* (London: Verso, 1983).

17. Joan Wallach Scott, *Gender and the Politics of History* (New York: Columbia University Press, 1988), p. 24.

18. Abd al-Rahim Mahmud, 1913–48, was from a small village near Nablus named *Anabta*. This line is from a poem in Harun Hashim Rashid, *al-Kalimah al-muqatilah* (Cairo: The Arabic Library, 1973), p. 15.

19. *Tomorrow is a Wonderful Day*, film directed by Helmar Lerski, produced by Hadassah, 1952.

20. Micha Josef Berdichevsky, cited in Ehud Luz, *Makbilim nifgashim*, (Parallels meet: religion and nationalism in the early Zionist Movement, 1882–1904), (Philadelphia: The Jewish Publication Society, 1988), pp. 167–9.

21. See description of the new man who can physically defend himself and family as the hope for the future of Jewish survival in an article by Moshe Shertok (Sharett), *Jewish Frontier Anthology 1934–44* (N.Y.: Jewish Frontier Association, 1945), pp. 328–35.

22. Fawaz Turki, 'Meaning in Palestinian history', *Arab Studies Quarterly*, vol. 3, no. 4, p. 374.

23. Darwazah, *al-Malak wa'l-Simsar*.

24. For a discussion of the life and work of Abd al-Rahim Mahmud, see Salma Jayyusi, *Anthology of Modern Palestinian Literature* (New York: Columbia University Press, 1992), p. 9.

25. Ibrahim Tuqan, *al-Shahid, al-Shir al-arabi fi ma'sat Filastin*, Kamal al-Sawafiri (ed.), (Cairo: Matba'a Nahda Misr, 1963), p. 225.

26. Leo Pinsker, 'Auto-emancipation: an appeal to his people by a Russian Jew', in B. Netanyahu (ed.), *Road to Freedom* (New York, 1944), pp. 15–42.

27. Amos Elon cites Yaari in *The Israelis: Founders and sons* (New York: Penguin Books, 1971), pp. 142–3.

28. A.D. Gordon, 1856–1922, born in Russia, emigrated to Palestine in 1904. This quote is from 'Some Observations', 1911, translated from Hebrew in Arthur Hertzberg (ed.), *The Zionist Idea: A historical analysis and reader* (New York: Doubleday Press, 1962), p. 375.

29. Martin Buber, 'An open letter to Mahatma Gandhi', *Israel and the World: Essays in a time of crisis* (New York: Schocken Books, 1948), p. 253.

30. Iskandar al-Khuri al-Baytjali, 1890–1973, poem written in 1918, translated in Khalid Sulaiman, *Palestine and Modern Arabic Poetry* (London: Zed Books, 1984), p. 19.

31. Ajaj Nuwiyhid, 'Kul Shabab' in *Filastin al-damiyyah, al-jarida al-jazir*, (Damascus: al-I'tidal Press, 1937) p. 107.

32. Khalid Sulaiman, *Palestine and Modern Arab Poetry* (London: Zed Books, 1984).

33. *Tomorrow is a Wonderful Day*, film directed by Helmar Lerski, produced by Hadassah, 1952.

34. Herzl, *Altneuland*, p. 75.

35. Arif al-Arif, *al-Nakbah* (Beirut: The Modern Library, 1947–52).

36. Muhammad Bindari, *al-Mar'a wa-markizaha al-ijtima'i fi'l-dawla* (Cairo: 1940s).

37. Kamal Mahmud Khalah observes the resistance to marry across class boundaries by urban dwellers who downgrade work on the land, in his study of documents of this period in *Filastin wa'l intidad al-Britani 1922–1939* (Palestine and the British Mandate 1922–1939) (Beirut: The P.L.O. Research Center, 1974), p. 12.

38. When these marriages did occur, the couples often lived within Arab communities.

39. Marie Syrkin, *Golda Meir: Woman with a cause* (1955, New York: Putnam and Sons, 1963), p. 318.

40. Syrkin, *Golda Meir*, p. 273.

41. Doris Katz, *The Lady was a Terrorist: During Israel's war of liberation* (New York: Shiloni, 1953), p. 140.

42. Herzl, *Altneuland*, p. 77.

43. Muhammad Jamil Bahim, *Fatat al-sharq* (Beirut, 1952).

44. Kumari Jayawardena, *Feminism and Nationalism in the Third World* (London: Zed Books, 1986), p. 12.

45. See A.L. Tibawi, *Arab Education in Mandatory Palestine: A study of three decades of British administration* (London: Luzac and Co., 1956) and Ruth Frances Woodsmall, *Moslem Women Enter a New World* (N.Y.: Round Table

46. Ylana Miller, *Government and Society in Rural Palestine 1920–1948* (Austin: University of Texas Press, 1985), p. 103.

47. Tibawi, *Arab Education*, p. 108.

48. Tibawi, *Arab Education*, pp. 228–9.

49. Lamya Baha al-Din, 'For the girls of today', *al-Difa*, 3 January 1944.

50. Ann Lesch, *Arab Politics in Palestine 1917–1939* (Ithaca: Cornell University Press, 1979), p. 57.

51. Noach Nardi, *Education in Palestine 1920–1945* (Washington: Zionist Organization of America, 1945), p. 153.

52. Nardi, *Education in Palestine*, p. 199.

53. Nardi, *Education in Palestine*, p. 173.

54. Norman Bentwich, *Palestine* (London: Ernst Benn, 1934), p. 254.

55. For a detailed analysis of the situation of some of these women see Deborah Bernstein, *The Struggle for Equality: Urban women workers in pre-state Israeli society* (N.Y.: Praeger, 1987) and *Pioneers and Homemakers: Jewish women in pre-state Israel* (New York: State University of New York Press, 1992).

56. Herzl, *Altneuland*, p. 75.

57. Matiel Mogannam, *The Arab Woman and the Palestine Problem* (London: Herbert Joseph, 1937 and Westport, CT: Hyperion Press, 1976).

58. Salwa Sardah, 'The woman's rights', *Sawt al-mar'a al-hur* (The Free Voice of Woman), no. 7 (1947).

59. See, for example, the account of women's efforts to take part in the decision-making process on Petah Tikva in Hannah Trager, *Pioneers in Palestine: Stories of the first settlers in Petach Tikva* (N.Y.: E.P. Dutton, 1924).

60. Many of these women's brief memoirs are collected in Katznelson-Shazar (ed.), *Divre Poalot*.

61. Violette Khoury, in Geraldine Stern (ed.), *Daughters from Afar: Profiles of Israeli women* (London: Abelard-Schuman, 1958), p. 35.

62. Molly Lyons Bar-David, *Women in Israel* (N.Y.: Hadassah Education Department, 1952), p. 95.

63. Atallah Mansour describes his mother's experiences, perceptions and convictions formed during her youth and then in his family during the mandate period in his autobiography, *Waiting for the Dawn* (London: Secker and Warburg, 1975).

64. Shifra Betzer, in Katnelson, *Divre Poalot*, p. 31.

65. Zipporah Seid, in Katznelson, *Divre Poalot*, p. 43.

66. Trager, *Pioneers in Palestine*, pp. 9 and 105.

67. Rachel Yanait Ben-Tzvi, *Before Golda, Manya Shohat: A biography*, (translated by Sandra Shurin, New York: Biblio Press, 1989), p. 90.

68. Malchah, in Katznelson, *Divre Poalot*, pp. 121–3.

69. See description of Jewish and Arab women nursing each others' children in Geoffrey Furlonge, *Palestine is My Country: Biography of Musa Alami* (London: John Murray, 1969), p. 6.

70. See memoirs of Geula Cohen, *Woman of Violence: 1943–1948*, trans. Hillel Halkin (New York: Holt Rinehart Winston, 1966), p. 107.

71. For example the involvement of Beatrice Magnes and Henrietta Szold in Brit Shalom. See Beatrice Magnes, *Episodes: A memoir* (Berkeley: Judah L. Magnes Memorial Museum, 1977) and Joan Dash, *Summoned to Jerusalem: The life of Henrietta Szold* (New York: Harper and Row, 1979).

72. Vladimir Jabotinsky, 1880–1940, born in Russia, leader of the Revisionist militant right-wing Zionists. This quote is from an address he gave to the House of Lords, 11 February 1937, as 'Evidence submitted to the Palestine Royal Commission' (pamphlet) p. 19.

73. Katz, *The Lady was a Terrorist*, pp. 12–13, and 108.

74. Benedict Anderson, *Imagined Communities*.

6

Gender and the Israeli–Palestinian Accord: Feminist Approaches to International Politics

Simona Sharoni

Long before the 1991 Madrid conference and the September 1993 signing of the Israeli–Palestinian Accord were under way, Palestinian and Israeli women engaged in a series of international peace conferences. The first such conference on the Israeli–Palestinian conflict entitled 'Give Peace a Chance—Women Speak Out' took place in May 1989 in Brussels. About fifty women—Israeli, Palestinian women from the West Bank and Gaza Strip and official representatives of the PLO met, for the first time in such a format, to discuss the Israeli–Palestinian conflict and the prospects for its resolution. Following the conference, in December 1989, representatives of the Palestinian Women's Working Committees and the Israeli Women and Peace Coalition co-co-ordinated a women's day for peace in Jerusalem which culminated in a march of 6,000 women from West to East Jerusalem under the banner 'Women Go For Peace'. These events were designed to alert the international community to the serious need for conflict resolution initiatives in the region and to develop feminist frameworks for peace-building in the Middle East.[1] Yet these international conferences and jointly organized activities remained unnoticed by gender-blind international media and by conflict resolution experts.

The secret negotiations which led to the formulation of the 'Gaza and Jericho First' plan, also known as the Oslo Accord, in September 1993 triggered numerous discussions concerning exclusions. Yet, while the media dealt extensively with the exclusion of both the United States and the Palestinian delegation from the process which led to the signing of the Accord, the exclusion of women from both secret and the official channels of negotiation remained unnoticed and unaddressed. What helps perpetuate and even naturalize this exclusion is the fact that the gendered assumptions, language and relations of power that underlie the Oslo Accord and its dominant representations remain concealed.

This chapter seeks to uncover some of the gendered practices, discourses and assumptions that were implicit in the Oslo Accord and which underscore, to a great extent, the study and practice of conflict resolution more generally. Drawing on particular examples from the recently signed accord between the Israeli government and the Palestine Liberation Organization (PLO), the paper proposes three possible feminist approaches designed to disrupt dominant representations of Middle East politics.[2]

The first approach takes issue with the exclusion of women and gender issues from both official and unofficial negotiation tables and with the marginalization of women's peace initiatives. The primary thrust of this approach is to create a level playing field by struggling for greater representation of women and their perspectives, in all their varieties, not only at the negotiation tables but at every level of the political arena. This approach which poses the question 'where are the women?' represents first and foremost a struggle for voice and visibility.

The second approach explores the differences between the voices and perspectives that mark conventional accounts of the Israeli–Palestinian conflict and those that are excluded or remain on the margins of these debates. It compares and contrasts the masculine–militarized language that characterizes the Israeli–Palestinian Accord with feminist understandings of peace and security that emerge from the daily lives and struggles of Israeli and Palestinian women. This approach calls attention to the central role gender plays in the construction of central understandings of identity and community and highlights the difference between masculinist and feminist interpretations of international politics.

Building upon the two previous approaches, the third calls for a critical examination of the underlying gendered assumptions of dominant accounts of the Israeli–Palestinian conflict and the prospects for its resolution. This approach begins with the premise that to make gender visible one must raise questions about taken-for-granted assumptions about masculinity, femininity and gender relations which underlie dominant accounts of world politics and international relations. By treating these assumptions as gendered, this intervention opens up space for a critical feminist inquiry into the processes, practices and prevailing power relations involved in the construction and adoption of these assumptions.[3]

Taken together, these approaches map out new horizons for feminist theorizing on international politics and outline new locations from which the Israeli–Palestinian conflict can be engaged with and theorized.

Making Gender Visible

If we employ only the conventional, ungendered compass to chart international politics, we are likely to end up mapping a landscape peopled only by men, mostly elite men. The real landscape of international politics is less exclusively male.[4]

Ever since the Madrid conference, the international media naturalized the absence of women at the negotiation tables by turning Hanan Mikhail-Ashrawi, the spokeswoman of the Palestinian delegation, into a media celebrity. Instead of calling attention to the striking absence of women involved in the negotiations, most accounts portrayed Dr Ashrawi as an exception, focusing on her intelligence, eloquence, and Western dress and education. Implicit in this representation was the assumption that talented, capable, Westernized women who understand the political game and learn how to play it do have a place and a voice in the arena of international politics. What most media accounts failed to recognize, however, was that Ashrawi, like Zahira Kamal and Suad Ameri, the other two women in the Palestinian delegation, 'earned' their places in the delegation due to the ongoing struggles of Palestinian women throughout the West Bank and Gaza Strip, especially since the outbreak of the Palestinian uprising, known as the *intifada*, in December 1987.[5]

As Cynthia Enloe points out, 'the national political arena is dominated by men but allows women some select access.'[6] In most cases the women who are able to enter or manage to 'invade' the arena of international politics have to be able to 'successfully play at being men, or at least not shake masculine presumptions'.[7] The women in the Palestinian delegation, however, had no motivation or intention to play this game. They do not resemble militaristic women leaders such as Margare Thatcher, Indira Gandhi, Jeanne Kirkpatrick and Golda Meir. On the contrary, one could argue that Hanan Ashrawi became a media celebrity in part because she introduced a unique perspective and a non-masculine voice to the arena of international politics. Ashrawi's popularity and success in presenting the Palestinian case to the international community may have been the major factor that prompted the appointment of women as spokespersons for the Syrian and Israeli delegations. On the surface, women's struggles for voice and visibility yielded positive results. Feminists, however, should celebrate these changes with both caution and suspicion, since they may indicate nothing more substantive than a contingent strategy of using women to 'sell' international politics. After all, it is almost always men who decide when women's visibility or invisibility is likely to benefit their national or international agendas. At the same time, in most cases, women's visibility or invisibility is not treated as an integral part of international politics and thus as worthy of investigation.

The following story confirms Enloe's assertion that 'women's roles in creating and sustaining international politics have been treated as if they were "natural" and thus not worthy of investigation.'[8] Following the signing of the Oslo Accord, one had to read between the lines of *The New York Times* and the Israeli press to find out that two prominent Norwegian women played a pivotal role in the pre-negotiation stage that led to the signing of the Israeli–Palestinian agreement.[9] The first is Marianne Heiberg, a scholar at FAFO, the Norwegian Institute for Applied Social Science, who is the author of a study of the living conditions in the Occupied Territories and also happened to be married to Johan Jorgen Holst, the Norwegian Foreign Minister, who got most of the credit for mediating the Oslo Accord. What remains largely unknown is that it was in fact Marianne Heiberg—using her connections in Israel and in the West Bank and Gaza Strip—who introduced both the Foreign Minister (her husband) and Terje Rod Larsen, the executive Director of FAFO (her boss), to key people on both the Israeli and Palestinian sides.

The second prominent woman whose role is even less known is Mona Yoll, who is the top advisor to the Norwegian Foreign Minister and also happens to be married to the Executive Director of FAFO, Terje Rod Larsen, the other man whose name and role in orchestrating the Accord became largely known. There are very few details about the exact role Mona Yoll played on the backstage of the secret negotiations in Oslo, but it is clear that she was instrumental in setting up the preliminary meetings that led to the direct secret negotiations and that she was present at most of these meetings. Her name and position, however, have been mentioned only in relation to her husband's, cited as evidence of the close connections that exist between FAFO and the Norwegian government.[10]

The marginalization of both Heiberg and Yoll's roles reveals that gender was a major factor in the process which led to the signing of the Oslo Accord; it determined who would be visible and who would remain invisible, whose services would get credit and whose would be taken for granted. The active roles these two prominent women played in the pre-negotiation stage remain the best-kept secrets in the history of the back-stage negotiation that led to the Accord.

'Making women invisible hides the working of both femininity and masculinity in international politics,' argues Enloe.[11] By calling attention to the power arrangements and the particular practices and processes involved in naturalizing women's invisibility in the arena of international politics, feminists can not only advance women's struggles for voice and visibility but also expose the gendered dimensions of world politics.[12] Thus, feminist struggles for voice and visibility do not begin and end with the reformist demand to 'add women' or 'listen to women'; they seek to create a broader context for the exploration of important questions concerning gendered discourses, taken-for-granted conceptions of masculinity, femininity, gender relations and practices of exclusion and inclusion that sustain the status quo in the arena of world politics.

Challenging the Discourse of Militarized Masculinity

> Perhaps international politics has been impervious to feminist ideas precisely because for so many centuries in so many cultures it has been thought of as a typically 'masculine' sphere of life.[13]

During the last week of August 1993 when news of the signing of Israeli–Palestinian Accord was made public, senior Middle East reporters and foreign policy media analysts, all men, packed their suitcases and rushed to Washington, DC. As a result, the gendered division of labour that characterizes Israeli media appeared to be changing as women reporters, who in the past had rarely been assigned to cover contemporary developments in international politics, were sent to the PLO headquarters in Tunis. Yet the change was only superficial since women were not assigned to write editorials, major news analyses or opinion pieces on the recently signed Accord; these assignments were covered by their male counterparts in Washington, DC. Rather, the 'women's squads' were sent to Tunis to capture the mood, interview Arafat's wife, and befriend PLO officials who stayed behind. In sum, women were assigned the task of finding the 'human' stories that will garnish the 'real' news that men are responsible for.

This telling anecdote supports Enloe's assertion that 'women's experiences...are relegated to the "human interest column".'[14] Evidently, not much has changed in the gendered arena of international politics since Simone de Beauvoir argued that 'representation of the world, like the world itself, is the work of men; they describe it from their own point of view, which they confuse with the absolute truth.'[15] It should not come as a surprise, therefore, that 'his' story of the Israeli–Palestinian Accord may be quite different from 'her's'. It would be a grave mistake, however, to invoke socio-biology to interpret these differences. Rather, as the second feminist approach explored in this paper suggests, the differences in the stories men and women tell about the Israeli–Palestinian Accord should not be treated as 'natural' but rather as socially constructed, reflecting different experiences, discourses and social locations.

According to Donna Haraway, a social location implies a 'view from a body, always a complex, contradictory, structuring, and structured body, versus the view from above, from nowhere, from simplicity'.[16] By problematizing the location from which men's dominant representations of international politics emerge, feminists not only make men visible as men, but also call into question particular configurations of power and privilege that underlie this location. Moreover, such an approach can map out alternative locations from which particular events in international politics can be engaged with and theorized. Haraway also points out that 'many currents in feminism attempt to theorize grounds for trusting especially the vantage points of the subjugated' since 'there is a good reason to believe vision is better from below the brilliant space platforms of the powerful.'[17] In a similar vein, Nancy Hartsock urges feminists 'to build an account of the world as seen from the margins, an account which can expose the falseness of the view from the top and can transform the margins as well as the center'.[18] In sum, women's voices and feminist perspectives, which have been ignored or marginalized in the study and practice of international politics, represent particular examples of what Foucault called 'subjugated knowledges'.[19]

The project of theorizing 'from below' is not merely an attempt to include the perspectives of the powerless and the excluded; it is a potentially transformative project that seeks to construct alternative accounts of social and political realities. In the context of the September 1993 Accord between the Israeli government and the PLO, theorizing 'from below' implies privileging accounts that emerge from the daily lives of women and from their struggles for a just and lasting resolution of the Israeli–Palestinian conflict. Such accounts have the potential to bring to the fore voices and perspectives that are presently missing from the dominant coverage of the Oslo Accord and more generally from conventional analyses of Middle East and international politics.

In her discussion of feminist theorizing that begins with the daily experiences of women, Sandra Harding stresses that:

> ...because women are treated as strangers, as aliens—some more so than others—by the dominant social institutions and conceptual schemes, their exclusion alone provides an edge, an advantage, for the generation of causal explanations of our social order from the perspectives of their lives.[20]

But it is not enough to recover submerged narratives grounded in women's lives and experiences. To ensure that these narratives are not trivialized, marginalized and confined to the 'human interest' columns, feminists should challenge dominant voices and discourses. As Carol Cohn argues:

> The dominant voice of militarized masculinity and decontextualized rationality speaks so loudly in our culture, [that] it will remain difficult for any other voices to be heard until that voice loses some of its power to define what we hear and how we name the world—until that voice is delegitimated.[21]

The gendered discourse of the Israeli–Palestinian Accord provides numerous examples of 'militarized masculinity' and 'decontextualized rationality'. Battlefield metaphors and warrior vocabulary were the central themes in Yitzhak Rabin's speech at the signing of the mutual declaration of principles between the Israeli government and the PLO on 13 September 1993. Consider, for example, Rabin's opening statement:

This signing of the Israeli–Palestinian declaration of principles here today—it's not so easy—neither for myself *as a soldier in Israel's war*, nor for the people of Israel, not to the Jewish people in the diaspora, who are watching us now with great hope mixed with apprehension. It is certainly not easy for *the families of the war's violence, terror, whose pain will never heal, for the many thousands who defended our lives as their own and have even sacrificed their lives for our own* [emphasis mine].[22]

Rabin is very clear about the identity and social location which inform his understanding of peace: he is first and foremost a soldier in Israel's war and the people of Israel and the Jewish people in the diaspora constitute his army. The warmonger of yesterday who turned a peacemaker overnight is clearly struggling not only with his new identity as a peacemaker but also with the need to justify past wars. Terms like victims, violence, terror, defence and sacrifice are utilized to constitute a narrative which assigns all the blame to 'the enemies' and thus frees Rabin, the soldier, from any responsibility for war and enables Rabin, the prime minister, to get the credit for peace.

This narrative and its gendered underpinnings are evident throughout the speech. For example, in the following paragraph Rabin asserts that :

We have come from a people, a home, a family that has not known a single year, nor a single month, *in which mothers have not wept for their sons. We* have come to try and put an end to the *hostilities* so that our children, our children's children, will no longer experience *the painful cost of war: violence and terror. We* have come to *secure* their lives...[emphasis mine].[23]

This paragraph is perhaps the most passionate in Rabin's speech, maybe even in his entire political career. Rabin the soldier is far from being a poet or a passionate speaker. He is known for his cynicism and for his direct, laconic manner of speech, which is often interwoven with military slang. Given this background, Rabin's mobilization of the image of mothers weeping for their sons and of 'our children' and 'our children's children' represents a cynical objectification of women and children for sheer nationalist propaganda. This type of objectification is quite common in Israel. As I have noted elsewhere, the funerals of Israeli soldiers, which are usually broadcast by the media, become politically charged as top government officials who attend the funerals are often shown comforting weeping mothers and commending them for raising sons who were ready to sacrifice their lives for their homeland.[24]

But government officials do not have a monopoly over the use of symbols associated with motherhood and with mother–son relations. Similar images have been utilized by women around the world, including women in Israel, to protest against the use of war and violence to solve problems and to hold government officials accountable for sending young people to die.[25]

Efrat Shpiegel is an Israeli mother whose son was killed during the Israeli invasion of Lebanon (1982–5) and who has since then been active in the Israeli peace movement. Yet, her analysis of war and understanding of peace is quite different from that presented by Rabin in the name of 'the mothers who have wept for their sons'. Shpiegel, who was very active against the Israeli invasion of Lebanon, points to the events and processes that shaped her life and political convictions:

> I began my own private peace campaign at the time of the Israel–Lebanon war. Until then I was one of the silent majority, with the attitude that no matter what I thought or felt, there was nothing I could do to change anything apart from exercising my right to vote every four years. With the Lebanon war, my attitude changed. My son Yo'av participated in that war. I had many talks with him about the war, I became involved. I started to closely examine what I heard, saw and read in the media. I started to suspect that I and thousands like me were being brainwashed, were being manipulated.[26]

One way to manipulate people is through an uncritical invocation of the pronoun 'we'. Indeed, 'we' appears more than twenty times in Rabin's speech. While in many instances the use of the term appears generic, a careful reading of the speech uncovers the particular 'we' that Rabin has in mind:

> *We, the soldiers who have returned from battles stained with blood; we,* who have seen our relatives and friends killed before our eyes; *we,* who have attended their funerals and cannot look in the eyes of their parents; *we,* who have come from a land where parents bury their children; *we,* who fought against you, the Palestinians [emphasis mine].[27]

Rabin's 'we' does not include people like Efrat Shpiegel, despite the fact that her personal loss and pain have been mobilized to construct a particular image of a cohesive Israeli/Jewish collectivity. In many ways, Rabin's 'we' does not include the majority of Israelis, with the exclusion of elite men who bear direct responsibility for Israel's wars. Rabin's 'we' is in fact an 'I', who cannot look Efrat Shpiegel in the eye for if he does, she will hold him directly accountable for her son's death. She will tell him that her son and 'thousands of young people like him on both sides were deprived of their lives, that her son "had died for nothing".'[28] Nevertheless, while the international community pays tribute to Rabin's courage to explore alternatives to war, Efrat Shpiegel's courageous struggle for peace remains unacknowledged. She who 'became an ardent protagonist of peace' despite the price she had to pay for 'war's tragic wastefulness and evil futility' is invoked by Rabin in his speech not as part of a larger 'we' of peace activists, but rather as an object to be manipulated, protected and secured.[29]

'Peace is my Security' reads a Peace Now banner at an October 1993 demonstration in support of the Oslo Accord. It is quite evident that, according to this slogan, peace is defined as the absence of war and security simply means 'national security'. Furthermore, through the use of the proposition 'my', Israel's security is privileged over the security of the entire region and its diverse citizenry. This will not come as a surprise to those familiar with both the origins and composition of Peace Now, the largest and most institutionalized segment of the Israeli Peace movement. Peace Now's leadership largely consists of high-ranking officers in the Israeli military who are either retired or on reserve and who go to great lengths to couch their positions on peace and conflict resolution within the discourse of national security.[30] Ironically, the pervasive discourse of 'national security' sets the parameters for dissent in Israel.

It has become the norm that to speak about peace requires that one is accepted as an authority on military strategy and on security, narrowly defined in military terms. As a result, Israeli women in general and women peace activists in particular have been further excluded from the centres of political debate. This particular practice of exclusion rests mainly on the fact that women's military training in Israel is not about preparing them to become experts on so-called 'national security' matters but is rather designed to ensure that women provide men with practical and moral support.[31] Israeli women are expected to fulfil this auxiliary role not only during their military service but also in society at large, and including the Israeli peace movement.

Hannah Safran, an Israeli feminist and peace activist, explains how the uncritical acceptance of the hegemonic discourse of 'national security' contributes to institutionalized sexism and works to disempower women within the peace movement:

> There are very powerful women in the movement but they are pushed to remain behind the scenes. . .Some stay in the movement despite the humiliation. I cannot tolerate this. I will not tolerate hierarchies built on military ranks in a peace movement. I don't care if he is a high-rank officer. I deserve to be treated as an equal human being and I refuse to continue and take part in male-dominated structures that are sustained under the pretext of so-called 'national security'.[32]

Given the pervasive intertwining of the Israeli peace movement with patriarchal structures within Israel, it is not surprising that Israeli women seized the opportunity to form their own organizations to express and act upon their political convictions. In many ways, the outbreak of the *intifada* did not simply trigger the emergence of a distinct women's peace movement in Israel, but also facilitated a search for alternative political discourses to articulate women's perspectives on the Israeli–Palestinian conflict.[33] Elsewhere, I have referred to these emerging perspectives as 'local feminist discourses'.[34]

What stands out about local feminist discourses is that they are not grounded in any one particular theory, nor directly informed by conflict resolution scholarship or by existing feminist frameworks on the relationship between women and peace. Rather, local discourses represent a search for a context-specific feminist standpoint, for a theory of struggle 'from below'. These discourses have emerged from and are grounded in particular experiences of struggle that have given rise to perspectives and interpretative frameworks which seek to relate feminist politics to the struggles to end the Israeli occupation of the West Bank and Gaza Strip and at the same time to end social injustice in Israel.

Local feminist discourses see the quest for peace and security as directly related to the eradication of various forms of oppression such as sexism, racism and homophobia; they reflect a strong and broadly conceived commitment to social and political change in the Middle East and around the world. As feminist peace activist Erella Shadmi points out:

> Oppression *per se* is my concern—whether of Palestinians, women, children, Sepharadic Jews, blacks or any other creature on earth. More-over, I am also very much concerned with fundamentalism,

environmental degradation, capitalism, compulsory heterosexuality and other ideologies which attempt to limit my liberty and free choice.[35]

Feminists who seek to challenge narrow and dominant formulations of peace and security and expose their masculinist-militaristic underpinnings, should turn to the growing body of feminist literature on peace and security.[36] Of particular importance in this context is an emerging body of feminist scholarship which explores alternative interpretations of peace and security that emerge from and have resonance in the daily lives and struggles of women in the Middle East and elsewhere.[37] But to open up space for alternative conceptualizations of peace and security it is not enough 'to give voice' to women peace activists or to highlight feminist perspectives on peace and security. Feminist scholars and activists must also raise questions concerning the often taken-for-granted assumptions which underlie dominant understandings of peace, security and conflict resolution and question their uncritical application to particular cases such as the Israeli–Palestinian Accord.

Gender Discourse and the Israeli–Palestinian Accord

Gender shapes not only who we are, how we live, play, and work, and what we have but also how we think, how we order reality, how we claim to know what is true, and, therefore, how we understand and explain the social world.[38]

The symbolic gesture of the hand-shake between Israeli Prime Minister Yitzhak Rabin and PLO Chairman Yasser Arafat on the South Lawn of the White House was presented as the crossing of a significant boundary, both politically and psychologically. Yet, at the same time, this uncritical and rather simplistic interpretation of a masculine hand-shake between official representatives of polities as a significant step toward conflict resolution reinforces the very boundary it claims to challenge: that between 'us' and 'them', between Israelis (and Jews) and Palestinians. The excessive (often obsessive) focus on both the actual and the symbolic significance of the hand-shake failed to mention, and indeed helped undermine, the ongoing struggles of women peace activists and other progressive social movements in the region for a just and lasting resolution of the Israeli–Palestinian conflict. This partial and simplistic representation of a peace accord is informed by a number of implicit gendered assumptions that ought to be made explicit and challenged.

The search for central assumptions, or 'webs of meaning' that underlie a particular body of scholarship involve epistemological and meta-theoretical questions. These are questions that address not only the content of particular knowledge claims, but also the processes and practices that inform their construction. In other words, theories and intervention models are assumed to be socially constructed rather than based upon unproblematic discoveries.[39] The search for 'webs of meaning' that has informed conventional accounts of the Israeli—Palestinian conflict and dominant representations of the Oslo Accord requires close attention to the prevalent social understandings and disciplinary assumptions which lead to the acceptance of particular knowledge claims.

The fact that a large number of scholars share some basic assumptions that frame a field of inquiry does not in any way imply that their work is deficient or compromised. Rather, the questions that need to be raised concern the degree to which the assumptions remain tacit and therefore unexamined and the extent to which other perspectives, which do not share the same assumptions, have been foreclosed by a particular framework. In what follows, I will try to make explicit the gendered dimensions of one central assumption that underlies most accounts of the Israeli—Palestinian conflict.

The central unchallenged assumption that informs most accounts of the Israeli—Palestinian conflict is that the conflict is between two major parties, Israelis and Palestinians. This view presupposes the existence of two cohesive, sovereign and unified parties locked into a conflict which manifests itself in the international arena as a conflict over territory. Based on this assumption in order to resolve the conflict, official representatives of the two parties have to be willing to come to the negotiation table. This assumption and the understandings of conflict and conflict resolution that it implies surfaces in the language of the Oslo Accord as well as in the speeches delivered at the 13 September 1993 ceremony. It is particularly evident in President Clinton's speech:

> As we all know, devotion to the land has been the source of conflict and bloodshed for too long. Throughout this century bitterness between the Palestinian and Jewish people has robbed the entire region of its resources, and too many of its sons and daughters...Today the leadership of Israel and the Palestine Liberation Organization will sign

a declaration of principles on interim Palestinian self-government...
let us today pay tribute to the leaders who had the courage to lead
their people toward peace, away from the scars of battle, the wounds
and the losses of the past, toward a brighter tomorrow.[40]

In addition to framing the discussion of who the actors in a
conflict are and how they are to be represented, the particular
formulation of a struggle between Israelis and Palestinians over
territory reduces the conceptualization of peace to an agreement
between enemies, a cliché that became Rabin's favourite.[41] One of
the reasons, in my opinion, that makes this simplistic formulation
so appealing to Rabin is that it allows him to reconcile his
masculine warrior identity with his pragmatic decision to sign the
Oslo Accord. Through the use of the banal cliché 'peace you
make with enemies, not with friends', Rabin puts forward a
formulation that has the connotation of a strong man's peace, an
agreement signed by a loyal soldier of the state, not by a 'soft'
(feminine) peace activist who can be dismissed as an 'Arab lover'.
Since 'peace', which is envisioned as the opposite of 'war', evokes
a feminine connotation, to maintain male control over this new
phase of politics Israel's security has always been mentioned in
conjunction with the term peace and references to the Israeli–
Palestinian Accord have often been imbued with overtly masculine,
militarized images.

To make visible the gendered dimensions of the assumption
that peace is made between enemies implies destabilizing and
denaturalizing other binary constructions such as strong/weak,
rational/irrational, public/private, order/disorder, stability/an-
archy, reason/emotion, war/peace. In each of these, gender is
insinuated into the terms, the first term being 'masculine' and
superior to its 'feminine' counterpart.[42] One should not confuse,
however, the central role of gender in the construction of binary
thinking with essentialized gender differences. That is, the thrust
of this argument is *not* that differences between men's and women's
thinking about war and peace originate from their maleness and
femaleness, but rather as Carol Cohn insists that 'gender discourse
intertwines with and permeates that thinking.'[43]

Many feminists have called attention to the fact that, while the
term gender refers to 'the constellation of meanings that a given
culture assigns to biological sex differences', the term 'gender
discourse' calls attention not only to words or language but also
to 'a system of meaning, of ways of thinking...that first shape how

we experience, understand and represent ourselves as men and women.'[44] Gender discourses inform, both implicitly and explicitly, our understanding of and relationship to questions of identity and community. That is, questions of who we are both as individuals and as part of an 'imagined community.'[45]

Rabin's interpretation of the Israeli—Palestinian conflict and of the Oslo Accord offer a very particular answer to the question of 'who we are'. As such it privileges a particular understanding of political community and identity based on the principle of state sovereignty. The centrality of the principle of sovereignty in dominant interpretations of identity and community has inspired conventional understandings of conflicts, in deeply divided societies and communities, as occurring between two sovereign parties. Therefore, it is particularly important to analyse what and who is included and excluded from these dominant understandings of 'the parties'.[46]

The conceptualization of the Israeli—Palestinian conflict as taking place between two sovereign, unitary actors, Israelis and Palestinians, has contributed to the exclusion of dissident voices in general and women's and feminists' voices in particular from conventional formulations of conflict. This particular form of exclusion has been further reinforced by the way in which most accounts of international politics approach questions of representation. To be considered 'representative' one has to be either a government official or within the mainstream of one's community.[47] What is problematic about this formulation is not the representative voices it includes, but rather those voices and perspectives which are considered to be outside the so-called 'mainstream of their communities', and as a result are excluded from the process of conflict resolution.

This practice of exclusion, like other social and political practices, is gendered. That is, people, practices, symbols and ways of thinking coded as 'masculine' mark the centre of politics, while what is rendered 'feminine' is relegated to the margins. This arbitrary distinction and the practices of exclusion it enables make 'the international system...look less complicated, less infused with power, less gendered than it really is.'[48] This practice is also informed by the rationale that representatives of the mainstream are likely to sway their communities in the direction of conflict resolution while people outside the mainstream are likely to complicate the process. This rationale tends to accept status quo formulations of what constitutes the *centre* and the *margins* of political life. As a result, the voices and perspectives of people and social movements in conflict areas as well as those of transnational groups—all of which are considered to be outside the mainstream—are left out of analyses.[49]

Lester Ruiz, however, emphasizes that those who inhabit the margins of supposedly sovereign communities are not without political agency. In fact, he argues that people who are part of 'critical social movements' or 'communities of resistance and solidarity', 'not only articulate a different understanding of political and ideological space, but also keep these spaces open for transformation.'[50] Feminist interpretations of the Israeli–Palestinian Accord can contribute both to the transformation and the enlargement of these spaces.

In making gender visible by disrupting the masculinist underpinnings of conventional accounts of international politics, feminist approaches provide examples of what politics might look like if the experiences and perspectives of women and of other subjugated groups were taken into consideration. By making explicit the gendered dimensions of central assumptions that frame conventional accounts of international politics, such as the signing of the Israeli–Palestinian Accord, feminist approaches expand the range of political, social and economic choices and understandings not only for women and for feminist theorizing but also for other groups whose voices and perspectives have been excluded or marginalized.

Notes

1. For more on the joint peace initiatives of Israeli and Palestinian women, see Naomi Chazan, 'Israeli women and peace activism' in Barbara Swirsky and Marilyn Safir (eds), *Calling the Equality Bluff: Women in Israel* (New York: Pergamon Press, 1991); Yvonne Deutsch, 'Israeli women: from protest to a culture of peace' in Deena Hurwitz (ed.), *Walking the Red Line: Israelis in search of justice for Palestine* (Philadelphia: New Society Publishers, 1992); Simona Sharoni, 'Gender and Middle East politics', *The Fletcher Forum of World Affairs*, vol. 17(2), Summer 1993: 59–73 and *Gender and the Israeli–Palestinian conflict: The politics of women's resistance* (Syracuse: Syracuse University Press, 1995).

2. The three types of feminist approaches presented here draw on Sandra Harding's typology of feminist epistemologies (empiricist, standpoint and post-modern) and more specifically Christine Sylvester's use of

this typology to look at the field of international relations through feminist lenses and on Linda Forcey's appropriation of this typology to outline the major arguments that mark women's relationship to questions of war and peace. See Sandra Harding, *The Science Question in Feminism* (New York: Cornell University Press, 1989); Christine Sylvester, 'The Emperors' theories and transformation: looking at the field through feminist lenses' in Dennis Pirges and Christine Sylvester (eds), *Transformations in Global Political Economy* (London: Macmillan, 1990); and Linda Forcey, 'Women as peacemakers: contested terrain for feminist peace studies', *Peace & Change*, 16(4): 331–54, 1991.

3. For an extensive discussion of this approach see Simona Sharoni, 'Conflict resolution through feminist lenses: theorizing the Israeli–Palestinian conflict from the perspectives of women peace activists in Israel', unpublished Ph.D. dissertation, George Mason University, August 1993.

4. Cynthia Enloe, *Bananas, Beaches & Bases: Making feminist sense of international politics* (Berkeley: University of California Press 1990), p. 1.

5. For detailed accounts of the struggles of Palestinian women in the West Bank and Gaza Strip since the outbreak of the *intifada* see for example Phillipa Strum, *The Women Are Marching: The second sex and the Palestinian Revolution* (New York: Lawrence Hill Books, 1992); Joost Hiltermann, *Behind the Intifada: Labor and women's movements in the Occupied Territories* (Princeton: Princeton University Press, 1991); Nahla Abdo, 'Women of the intifada: gender, class and national liberation', *Race & Class*, 32(4) (1991): 19–34; Suha Sabbagh, 'Palestinian women writers and the Intifada', *Social Text*, 22 (Spring 1989): 1–19; and Samira Haj, 'Palestinian Women and Patriarchal Relations', *Signs: Journal of Women in Culture and Society*, 17(4) (Summer 1992): 761–78; and Simona Sharoni, *Gender and the Israeli–Palestinian Conflict*.

6. Enloe, *Bananas, Beaches & Bases*, p. 13.

7. Ibid.

8. Ibid., p. 4.

9. Stephen Engelberg, 'For the unlikely middleman from Norway, public thanks', *The New York Times*, 14 September 1993, p. A4; Alon Pinkas, 'Jerusalem–Oslo–Tunis: the crystallization of the Accord', *Ma'ariv*, 3 September 1993, pp. 4–5 (Hebrew); Nachum Barnea and Shimon Shifer, 'The Norwegian connection', *Yediot Achronot*, pp. 2–3 (Hebrew).

10. See *Yediot Achronot*, 10 September 1993, p. 22 (Hebrew).

11. Enloe, *Bananas, Beaches & Bases*, p. 11.

12. For a discussion of masculinity in international politics see Jane L. Parpart and Marysia Zalewski (eds), *The Man Question in International Relations* (Boulder: Westview, forthcoming).

13. Enloe, *Bananas, Beaches & Bases*, p. 11.

14. Ibid., p. 4.

15. Simone de Beauvoir, *The Second Sex* (New York: Knopf, 1952), p. 161.

16. Donna Haraway, 'Situated knowledges: the science question in feminism and the privilege of partial perspective', *Feminist Studies*, 14(3) (Fall 1988), p. 589.

17. Haraway, 'Situated knowledges', p. 583.

18. Nancy Hartsock, 'Foucault on power: a theory for women?' in Linda Nicholson (ed.), *Feminism/Postmodernism* (New York: Routledge, 1990), p. 171.

19. Michel Foucault, *Power/Knowledge: Selected interviews and other writings, 1972–1977* (New York: Pantheon, 1980), pp. 81–2.

20. Sandra Harding, *Whose Science? Whose Knowledge? Thinking from women's lives* (New York: Cornell University Press, 1991), p. 125.

21. Carol Cohn, 'Sex and death in the rational world of defense intellectuals' in Linda Rennie Forcey (ed.), *Peace: Meanings, politics, strategies* (New York: Praeger, 1989), p. 64.

22. Excerpt from Rabin's speech as reprinted in *The New York Times*, 14 September 1993, p. A12.

23. Ibid.

24. Simona Sharoni, 'Every woman is an Occupied Territory: the politics of militarism and sexism and the Israeli–Palestinian conflict', *Journal of Gender Studies*, 1(4), November 1992: 447–62.

25. For a detailed discussion of the images and politics of motherhood in the context of the Israeli–Palestinian conflict see Simona Sharoni, 'Motherhood and the politics of women's resistance: the case of Israeli women organizing for peace' in Annelise Orleck and Diana Tylor (eds), *Radical Motherhood: Mothers, politics and social change in the 20th century* (The University of England Press, forthcoming).

26. Efrat Shpiegel, 'A bereaved mother speaks', *Challenge*, 3(5), 1990, p. 12.

27. *The New York Times*, 14 September 1993, p. A12.

28. Shpiegel, 'A bereaved mother speaks', p. 12.

29. Ibid.

30. Peace Now generally supports the Labour Party's vague formulation of 'territorial compromise' for peace and endorsed Shimon Peres's efforts to implement the Jordanian option, that is to establish a Palestinian state in the West Bank and Gaza Strip. In addition, while Peace Now recognized in principle the Palestinian people's right to self-determination, it has not demanded the establishment of an independent Palestinian state and has never advocated Israeli withdrawal from all the territories occupied in 1967. Peace Now also echoed the national consensus in Israel on the question of Jerusalem by supporting the annexation of the city and stressing the need to maintain its 'unified' nature. For more on the responses of Peace Now and other groups on the Israeli left to the *intifada* see Reuven Kaminer, 'The protest movement in Israel' in Zachary Lockman and Joel Beinin (eds), *Intifada: The Palestinian uprising against Palestinian*

occupation (Boston: South End Press & MERIP, 1989: 231–45) and Stanley Cohen, 'The Intifada in Israel: portents and precarious balance', *Middle East Report*, 164–5 (May-August 1990): 16–20.

31. For more on the military service of Israeli women see Nira Yuval–Davis, *Israeli Women and Men: Divisions behind the unity* (London: Change Publications, 1982); Anne Bloom, 'Women in the defence forces' in *Calling the Equality Bluff*, pp. 128–38 and Sharoni, *Gender and the Israeli–Palestinian Conflict*, pp. 41–7.

32. An excerpt from my conversation with Hannah Safran, May 1990, Haifa, Israel.

33. Sharoni, *Gender and the Israeli–Palestinian Conflict*.

34. Sharoni, 'Conflict resolution through feminist lenses', pp. 223–30.

35. Erella Shadmi, 'Politics through the back door', *Women in Black National Newsletter*, no. 2 (Spring 1992), p. 7.

36. For recent important contributions to this body of literature, see for example Ann Tickner, *Gender in International Relations: Feminist perspectives in achieving global security* (New York: Columbia University Press, 1992); Rebecca Grant, 'The quagmire of gender and international security' in V. Spike Peterson (ed.), *Gendered States: Feminist (Re)Visions of International Relations Theory* (Boulder, CO: Lynne Rienner Press, 1992); V. Spike Peterson, 'Security and sovereign states: what is at stake in taking feminism seriously?' in *Gendered States*; Betty Reardon, *Women and Peace: Feminist Visions of Global Security* (New York: SUNY Press, 1993); Christine Sylvester, 'Riding the hyphens of feminism, peace and place in four- (or more) part cacophony', *Alternatives*, 18 (1), Winter 1993: 109–18.

37. For recent examples of feminist theorizing based on women's struggles in the Middle East see for example Judith Tucker (ed.), *Arab Women: Old boundaries, new frontiers* (Bloomington & Indianapolis: Indiana University Press, 1993) and Simona Sharoni, 'Middle East politics through feminist lenses: toward theorizing international relations from women's struggles', *Alternatives*, 18(1), Winter 1993: 5–28. For feminist literature on women's struggles in other parts of the world see other contributions to the same issue of *Alternatives*, a special issue edited by Christine Sylvester under the title, *Feminists Write International Relations*. In addition to the Israeli–Palestinian conflict, articles address from different feminist perspectives recent political developments in South Africa, Kenya and Europe and discuss their implications for women's lives and struggles.

38. V. Spike Peterson, 'The politics of identity in international relations', *The Fletcher Forum of World Affairs*, 17(2), Summer 1993, p. 7.

39. For further discussion of the epistemological and meta-theoretical questions that need to be addressed as part of the project of identifying and challenging particular 'webs of meaning' and central assumptions, see for example Richard Bernstein, *The Restructuring of Social and Political Theory* (New York: Harcourt Brace Jovanovich, 1976) and *Beyond Objectivism*

and Relativism: Science, hermeneutics, and praxis, (Philadelphia: University of Pennsylvania Press, 1983). See also Charles Taylor, 'Interpretation and the science of man', *Review of Metaphysics*, 25, 1971: 3–51, reprinted in Paul Rabinow and William M. Sullivan (eds), *Interpretive Social Science: A second look* (Berkeley: University of California Press, 1987).

40. *The New York Times*, 14 September 1993, p. A12.

41. Rabin used the cliché: 'Peace you make with enemies' on a few occasions, including at the Labor Party meeting that was assembled to ratify the agreement and in the Israeli Parliament debate prior to the vote on the agreement. See 'Rabin: Peace is made with enemies, even if they are despicable', *Yediot Achronot*, 3 September 1993, p. 4 (Hebrew).

42. For further discussion of this point in reference to feminist theorizing in international relations see Anne Sisson Runyan and V. Spike Peterson, 'The radical future of realism: feminist subversions of international relations theory', *Alternatives*, 16 (1991): 67–106; V. Spike Peterson, 'Transgressing Boundaries: Theories of knowledge, gender and international relations', *Millennium: Journal of International Studies*, 21(2), 1992: 183–206 and V. Spike Peterson and Anne Sisson Runyan, *Global Gender Issues* (Boulder, CO: Westview Press, 1993).

43. Carol Cohn, 'Wars, wimps, and women: talking gender and thinking war' in Miriam Cooke and Angela Wollacott (eds), *Gendering War Talk* (Princeton, NJ: Princeton University Press, 1993), p. 229.

44. Ibid., pp. 228–9.

45. Benedict Anderson, *Imagined Communities* (New York: Verso, 1983).

46. For critiques of the centrality of the principle of sovereignty see R.B.J. Walker, 'Sovereignty, Identity, Community: Reflections on the Horizons of contemporary political practice' in R.B.J. Walker and Saul Mendlovitz (eds), *Contending Sovereignties: Redefining Political Community* (Boulder, CO: Lynne Rienner Publishers, 1990, 159–85).

47. For an extensive discussion of this problematic see Sharoni, 'Conflict resolution through feminist lenses', pp. 73–81.

48. Enloe, *Bananas, Beaches & Bases*, p. 199.

49. R.B.J. Walker, *One World, Many Worlds: Struggles for a just world peace* (Boulder, CO: Lynne Rienner Publishers, 1988).

50. Lester Edwin Ruiz, 'Sovereignty as transformative practice' in Walker and Mendlovitz (eds), *Contending Sovereignties*.

7

Women's Writing in Egypt: Reflections on Salwa Bakr

Hoda El Sadda

In a conference on Arabic Literature held in 1992 at Cairo University, Salwa Bakr,[1] one of the most prominent contemporary Egyptian writers, objected to the blatant marginalization of women writers in the conference exemplified by the absence of the name of a single woman writer in the closing session scheduled for the following day. The organizers responded to her objection promptly, yes, but with a touch of humorous indulgence, by inviting her to take part in the final panel of eminent writers. Sure enough, Salwa Bakr appeared at the session and took her place on the panel amidst conflicting views about whether she should have accepted or rejected a half-hearted invitation. Addressing an audience of academics, writers and students, she asked them to bear with her, for her speech had been written in the brief interval she had between clearing the breakfast table and setting the table again for lunch. The majority of the audience did not appreciate her remark. Yet, as she proceeded to unravel the strata of experience which she believed were significant moments in her journey towards maturity, she captured their attention. Still, a young academic was heard whispering: 'If only she hadn't ruined the introduction by referring to the "trivial" details of a woman's daily life!'

This comment touches the core of the precarious position occupied by Arab women writers in the world of literature. If they want to be writers they must rise to the challenge of a literary tradition that refuses to recognize the specificities of a woman writer's vision. Phrases such as 'woman writer', 'woman's literature', 'woman's point of view' are summarily dismissed for their lack of seriousness. Literature is not gendered. Good literature is objective and universal; it crosses the boundaries of time, place, race and gender, as the saying goes. In the absence of a strong feminist critical tradition, women writers in Egypt and the Arab world are still intimidated by the male-dominated critical establishment which is as yet very intolerant of them. Such critics condemn women writers for producing 'women's literature' or 'feminist literature' and only commend a woman writer for rising above the petty prejudices of her sex and the narrow confines of her subjectivity in order to soar into the realms of the 'universal' and the 'objective' and write about the world from the point of view of all of 'mankind'. The point is, of course, that terms such as 'universal', 'humanity' and 'mankind', far from really encompassing both men and women, actually represent a world view dominated by a male perspective on culture in which women are marginalized and denied participation or expression. To gain recognition in the literary cultural scene, women are required to assimilate and reproduce the dominant male discourse, i.e. to write from the perspective of men or 'mankind'.

Nevertheless, Salwa Bakr is gaining standing and recognition because she has succeeded in developing a voice of her own. Her voice problematizes many of the cultural and literary givens about men and women, about the role of the artist in the Third World, about objectivity and subjectivity and about language. She rewrites the ground rules of cultural discourse by rejecting the basic assumptions that are put forward as natural givens and offers an alternative, protean image of social and gender relations that contribute to the dismantling of conventional values, structures and relationships. Her achievement can only be fully appreciated within a feminist analytical framework and within the context of other women writers in Egypt.

Analytical Approaches to Women's Writing

In a pioneering study, Elaine Showalter[2] divides the progress towards maturity of women's consciousness in their quest for self-fulfilment and cultural assertion into three stages: the Feminine, the Feminist and the Female. She traces the development of women's writing as represented in these stages in an attempt to understand the differences in view between women writers.

'Feminine' refers to an early stage of awareness in which women resent their disadvantaged position in relation to men but are as yet unable historically and culturally to suggest other relations, an alternative. Products of an exclusively male-dominated culture, they have internalized the prevalent assumptions about their 'female' nature and consequently perpetrate and implement existing stereotypes about women and the conventional roles which they are expected to fulfil. Products of this early stage, awed by the literary, intellectual and scientific achievements of men and as yet unable to formulate a coherent discourse about the cultural and historical conditions that resulted in the subordination of women, they decide to compete with men on their own terms, to equal or better their achievements and hence gain access to the literary tradition. At the 'Feminist' stage, women writers are able, historically and culturally, through their newly acquired access to the world of letters to voice their rejection of all the institutions, traditions and individuals implicated in one way or another in the saga of the subjection of women. In the 'Female' stage, women 'reject both imitation and protest—two forms of dependency— and turn instead to female experience as the source of an auto-nomous art, extending the feminist analysis of culture to the forms and techniques of literature.'[3]

Showalter's analysis of the 'Feminine' stage offers a convincing response to a worrying question: how come many women writers reproduce and recycle the same structures of thought that oppress them? In her article 'Are women's novels feminist novels?'[4] Rosa-lind Coward has pointed out that the Mills and Boon romances which reaffirm and popularize extremely regressive images of women entrapped in social, racial and sexual discrimination, are written by women and read by women. As Showalter has indic-ated, writing by women in this early stage of awareness need not differ from writing by men. The following 'Feminist' stage cor-responds to the revolutionary stage in the feminist movement when women, as a reaction to their long subjugation, strongly attack the male establishment and male culture. Showalter then faces a difficult impasse when she reaches the 'Female' stage. In this stage, women have gained sufficient awareness to enable them to see through the systems of thought that enslaved them. They are now relatively free to express 'female experience'. The question re-mains: what are the characteristics of female experience? Do all women share the same female experience? More significantly, do women writers possess the necessary tools for representing their experience?

We find ourselves back at square one. In a later article, Showalter investigates the possibility of defining the unique dif-ference of women's writing and asks: is the difference 'biological, linguistic, psychoanalytic, [or] cultural?'[5] She proceeds to analyse the theoretical assumptions of key texts in American feminist criticism such as Gilbert and Gubar's *The Mad Woman in the Attic*, Adrienne Rich's *Of Women Born* and others.

A discussion of the characteristics of women's writing necessarily leads to French theories of '*l'écriture féminine*' epitomized in the writings of Hélène Cixous and Luce Irigaray. Both Cixous and Irigaray have produced '*textes féminins*' using a language that defies accepted norms and that purports to draw upon the unique experience of a woman's body. In her manifesto of *l'écriture féminine*, 'The laugh of the Medusa',[6] Cixous argues that there is an essential difference between men and women at the level of sexual pleasure that needs to find expression in women's writing. Consequently, women's writing only becomes truly liberating and different when it defies the structures of thought and feeling imposed on women by the phallocentric logic embedded in the language we use.

Although this is an attractive argument, in as much as it offers hope for constructing an alternative discourse, it remains highly problematic. Not only is it essentialist but it also eludes the numerous differences between different women's experiences around the world. As Ann Rosalind Jones suggests, 'we need to ask not how Woman is different from Man,...[but] how women have come to be who they are through history.'[7]

This leads us to another French feminist theorist, Julia Kristeva, who modifies the notion of an essentially biological '*écriture féminine*' by arguing that the difference between men and women lies in the different way they internalize the 'socio-symbolic contract'.[8] In other words, the difference lies in the marginal position occupied by women in relation to the patriarchal symbolic order. This idea allows feminist criticism to escape from the impasse of essentialism and to investigate processes of becoming that take into consideration social and historical contingencies. This position is adopted by Toril Moi who defines feminist criticism as 'a specific kind of political discourse...committed to the struggle against patriarchy and sexism.'[9] What distinguishes feminist criticism is not its object of study—women's writing or female characters—but its stand against dominant male-centred culture. Similarly, Showalter, after reviewing various critical models for analysing women's writing, advocates a cultural model that interprets perceptions of women's body, psyche and language against the social context in which they occur. In this way, women's writing 'can be read as a double-voiced discourse, containing a dominant and a muted story'.[10] The conflict between the dominant and the muted voices re-enacts the marginalized position of women *vis-à-vis* the dominant culture. The specificity of women's writing can be studied in this space of tension created by the slanted perception of dominant modes through the eyes of a marginalized woman.

It is unlikely that the debate over the definitive differences in women's writing will exhaust itself so long as the basic problem of gender discrimination persists. Nevertheless, the force and magnitude of the feminist movement in the West has extracted an acknowledgement of two central issues: first, that there is such a thing as women's writing that has been systematically marginalized and hence needs to be given adequate critical attention and second, that women's writing is potentially capable of projecting representations of the world and of experiences that are different from those emanating from male authors. Given these two points of departure, critics argue and disagree about kinds of difference, theoretical and philosophical assumptions and other priority issues.

Women's Writing in Egypt

In Egypt, however, the debate over women's writing still revolves around whether the term is justifiable or not, and whether women experience life in different ways. The women's movement in Egypt has not, so far, been effective enough to establish new critical trends in the cultural field.

The first generation of Egyptian women writers, prominent among whom are Suhair al-Qalamawy and Amina Sa'id, stormed the cultural scene in the 1930s and 1940s and had distinguished careers in a hostile atmosphere peopled by men intolerant of such intrusive women. Pioneers in every sense of the word, these women writers accepted the already existing rules formulated by men of letters and hence represent the 'Feminine' stage, as described by Showalter. The 1950s and 1960s saw the payoffs of the national project for the education of women in the appearance of a generation of numerous professional women who occupied key positions in the world of culture. This is the generation of Iqbal Baraka, Sekina Fouad and Nawal El Saadawi, who were enabled by some of these new-found gains to express their rejection of the male-dominated culture that subordinated women. Nawal El Saadawi, the most famous, even notorious exponent of the more aggressive

'Feminist' stage, has enjoyed considerable fame in the Arab world and in the West but has remained significantly marginal in Egypt. She has displayed both courage and initiative in her vehement assault on male domination, patriarchal society and all forms of authority that buttress the subordination of women. Nevertheless, her exclusion from the Egyptian cultural scene epitomizes the marginality of the women's movement in Egypt and its inability to make space for dissident and militant voices.

The 1970s and 1980s have witnessed the rise of new voices that seek to explore the specificity of women's perspectives. These attempts, however, are not symptomatic of a vibrant and active theoretical environment that has created space for gender-sensitive writing and criticism. Women writers cannot assume the existence of common ground or a common language in a general discussion of women's writing or the position of women writers. They will often enough find themselves stuck at the basics, trying to convince their audience that writing from the point of view of women is a real possibility and not a hypothetical fantasy.

Showalter's stages in the development of women's writing, 'Feminine', 'Feminist' and the 'Female', all co-exist in the contemporary Egyptian scene. The current situation of literary women is an inevitable reflection of the setbacks suffered by women in their effort to gain more rights. Following the promotion of women's demands in the 1950s and 1960s, their achievement of constitutional rights and social esteem, women were among the first sections of society to bear the brunt of the collapse of the post-independence national project. The confusion of ideologies that prevailed in the 1970s, the alienation experienced by many at the loss of the national dream of progress, the stark discrepancies in wealth that became very visible in the 1980s, and the gradual (consequent) spread of religious fanaticism resulted in reverses and contestations over the position of women in Egyptian society. Together these setbacks have necessarily cast their shadow on the literary scene; the same old battles are fought over and over again and the same debates are tediously thrashed out in the media. In 1988 Suhair al-Qalamawy, in an introduction to an anthology of short stories by women writers, still felt compelled to assert that there is no such thing as:

> ...women's literature, there is only one literature that deals with various themes, one of these might be women, written by men and women

alike. I was therefore pleased to find that all the writers (women) included in this anthology express common problems that touch society as a whole, and the individual as a human being, be he a man or a woman.[11]

Al-Qalamawy expresses a common enough sentiment: if women want to gain recognition in a man's world they have to assimilate and reproduce the dominant discourse

The Contribution of Salwa Bakr

Salwa Bakr manages to go beyond this limitation. As she says in an interview:

> I do not believe that man is responsible for the unhappiness of woman. I hold responsible the structure of relations, the social specifications, concepts, values and prevalent norms. I deliberately portrayed man with no distinct features as a marginalized figure...I do not condemn man as a race or a sex but I do condemn the overall shape of our lives, the preconceived ideas which we accept as natural givens though they are not so, and should not be so. I condemn the common, the familiar, the taken-for-granted.[12]

Salwa Bakr's stories are not directed against men, a fact which has earned her the admiration and approval of many critics[13] who are harshly dismissive of any woman writer who shows signs of taking up such themes. Yet, contrary to the belief of these critics, Salwa Bakr writes in this way not just because she cherishes the 'universality' of values that are common to all humankind, but because she does not confine herself to what Hélène Cixous has described as 'dual, hierarchical oppositions'.[14] Drawing upon Derrida's deconstruction of Western metaphysics in which thoughts and concepts always work through a network of hierarchical binary oppositions, Cixous constructs a long list of dichotomous pairs of concepts that are commonly used to qualify each other and in which the first term is always accorded a position of dominance and hegemony, at least preference, in relation to the second as in 'Activity/Passivity, Sun/Moon, Culture/Nature, High/Low, Nature/Mind, Master/Slave, and ultimately Man/Woman'.[15] Consequently, and as Toril Moi suggests, for a woman writer 'to continue advocating binary thought, implicitly or explicitly, would seem to be tantamount to remaining inside patriarchal metaphysics'.[16]

It is to Salwa Bakr's credit that despite the highly oppressive environment in which she lives, her work comes through as a significant revision of conventional, stereotyped structures and relations. She transcends the limits of binary thought in her search for alternative structures, images and relations that will ultimately prove to be more liberating and more fulfilling for women and men. Salwa Bakr's fiction defies any reductive attempt at classification or categorization. She succeeds in doing so by refusing to depict 'the struggle of the sexes' through situating her women characters in the larger context of subjugation and enslavement which is the fate of individuals forced to submit to a life of drudgery and social inequality; by giving voice to the unheard voices of underprivileged women from the lower classes of society; by undermining the traditional roles of women and emphasizing their limitless potential outside the seclusion of their homes; by deconstructing the opposition between public and private spheres traditionally used to exclude women from public concerns and affairs and limit them to their domestic reality, and by constructing a new language to express her original vision.

Salwa Bakr depicts the lives of women, the majority of whom belong to the lower classes, hence bearing the burden of maximum oppression. 'Noony the loony' is the story of a thirteen-year-old servant girl. She quenches her thirst for the education she has never had by listening in on snatches of lessons conducted in a school next door. When her father suddenly appears to take her home to be married to a rich suitor, she escapes. The young girl is not only a victim of paternal authority, she is also, at the same time, a victim of social injustice that has gradually accumulated across years of political and economic blunders. The predicament of those forced to fend for themselves under disgraceful conditions which deprive them of their humanity comes to a head in the person of Noony who stands at the bottom of the social ladder: not only is she a girl owned by her family, but she is also a poor, illiterate, lowly servant girl with nothing to fall back on save her own resources. Noony's strength and initiative stem from her innate intelligence, her inquisitive mind that shields her from becoming just another passive recipient of preconceived ideas and values. She stands in front of the mirror and searches for the 'pupil of the eye' which the school teacher mentions. She wonders about the meaning of the mesmerizing words she hears repeated by the schoolgirls. In contrast to the lazy, stupid son of the mistress of the house, she appreciates and craves for knowledge as a possible means for self-betterment. Her escape at the end allows for multiple possibilities, of which one is success.

In another story 'Mother of Shehta triggers the whole affair', a washer-woman displays more initiative and political awareness than the educated, leftist intellectual, Hussein Diab, who is dumb-founded by her actions and her ingenuity. The story is told against the background of what came to be known as the Bread Riots, which erupted in 1977 after the government raised the price of bread and other basic goods overnight. Threatened by the consequent loss of her daily sustenance and armed by her common sense and innate fearlessness, she takes to the streets, gradually gathering a huge crowd of women and marches towards the representatives of government authority to talk them into retracting their decision. This active demonstration by illiterate women motivated by their practical needs and no-nonsense logic is highlighted by being contrasted to the ineffectual, passive and futile intellectual debates propagated by the so-called progressive left and concretized in the figure of Hussein Diab. An exponent of leftist slogans and clichés about the future role of the proletariat in the coming struggle for social and political freedom, about the alleged powerlessness and ineptitude of the people at this moment in history when faced with an organized armed force, Hussein Diab's propagandist rhetoric is exposed as fraudulent and ultimately regressive. Salwa Bakr shatters labels and pre-set tags hooked on to individuals: shrewdness and foresight are not the sole property of the educated. Whereas, after the riots, Hussein Diab returns to his room and is, naturally, arrested by the police, Mother of Shehta disappears for a couple of days until things quiet down.

In 'Sleeping on the more comfortable side', Fatma, a servant girl who has just given birth, fearing for her job resumes her work in the service of Sophie without taking adequate rest. As an act of kindness and a sign of appreciation, Sophie, a typical middle-class, idle woman gives Fatma a book about child care to help her raise her baby. After labouring through the book (for she can barely decipher words) and reading about the quantity of diapers and other clothes that a baby needs, about the necessity of applying cream after each feeding, Fatma stops and wonders about the credibility and viability of all the advice and instructions on offer. Depending on her common sense and practical experience, she comes to the conclusion that the whole book and its contents are sheer rubbish, and that Sophie is a simpleton for complying with its bizarre rules. Her reasoning is further confirmed by her keen observing eye as she recalls Sophie's two ill-mannered and spoilt daughters, the obvious products of modern methods of child upbringing. Fatma's wisdom and insight is set against Sophie's uncritical acceptance of fads and fashions and conventional patterns of behaviour. Again, we discover that the simple, almost illiterate servant girl has more potential for change than the established and affluent middle-class woman who is totally brainwashed by the status quo and by the privileges she enjoys. Sophie's enslavement as a woman and an individual is humorously exposed when she parrots the official discourse about the importance of birth control, only to fall on the deaf ears of clever Fatma who responds with a playful mimicry of formal style.

In 'Zeinat at the President's funeral', we meet one of Salwa Bakr's most interesting characters. A poor woman who lives in the streets in a little dilapidated shack, Zeinat comes through as a vibrant embodiment of the euphoric dreams and hopes of the whole post-revolution generation, the subsequent collapse of those dreams and the consequent disillusionment that followed. The story is about Zeinat who regularly corresponds with the President (Nasser) whom she considers her only living friend and supporter. She is granted social security money which she uses to devise a development plan to raise her standard of living. Zeinat's naive faith in the sincerity and genuine concern of the President for poor people like her is ironically problematized by the poignant description of the shabbiness of Zeinat's living conditions and by the squads of seemingly ordinary men in civilian dress who are actually armed to the teeth with weapons stashed in their black leather boots and who beat up Zeinat when she tries to approach the President. The story reaches it climax when Zeinat receives news about the President's death. Distracted and bewailing her ill fortune, she marches in his funeral procession and is again beaten up and arrested for attempting to touch his coffin. In the last paragraph, we are told, she joins in the Bread Riots which occurred later in the Sadat era and in which she repeatedly bewailed the death of her real supporter, Nasser. Political awareness, as this story suggests, is no longer a matter for the well-off, educated, privileged middle class with enough leisure time to show a civilized interest in affairs of state and national issues.

Salwa Bakr smoothly fuses the public and private spheres by her portrayal of a simple, uneducated woman whose personal life is inevitably part and parcel of larger conflicts. Active participation in the political scene in the case of Zeinat, like the mother of Shehta, is a matter of life and death. She notices the incongruent presence of the armed men wearing black boots but ascribes this ugly manifestation of the police state to the President's entourage, still holding on to her dream. Yet, the following era in which all the contradictions, the mistakes and frustrations jump to the surface of everyday life compels her to take a positive stand and she does.

Faiza in 'A woman in love' is the prototype of a married woman caught up 'like an ox harnessed to a water wheel' in the eternal mesh of complex responsibilities. The story recreates in a very rhythmic style the daily chores Faiza has to do at work and at home, leaving her at the end of the day completely drained. The only time she snatches a joyful moment is at night when she dreams of a mythical lover who rescues her. Although Faiza's dream is an escapist paradise, it nevertheless enables her to triumph over her destiny symbolically represented in the 'eternal' smile stamped on her face, in her tolerance and good-natured management of other people's problems.

In 'Such a beautiful voice that comes from within her', Salwa Bakr resorts to another, very effective, symbolic device to represent her main character's potential for achievement and for self-assertion. Sayeda, a lower-class, uneducated housewife and the mother of a gang of children, wakes up one morning to the realization that she possesses a beautiful voice, 'unlike the voice of the Sayeda she knows'. This realization awakens in her deeply suppressed needs and desires that have never been allowed to come up to the surface of her consciousness, strapped as she is to her daily routine of never-ending housework. Ridiculed by her husband and frowned upon by the neighbourhood grocer, Sayeda is finally escorted by a concerned husband to consult a psychiatrist. Hoping that an educated man might after all acknowledge her new-found treasure, she tries to sing a little song to the psychiatrist only to be silenced by a stern glance. He prescribes tranquillisers and anti-depressants, dismissing the whole affair as a case of temporary depression, a touch of madness. Battered on all fronts and unable to find space for her pent-up aspirations, Sayeda loses her beautiful voice and goes back to her same old self. The story ends when Sayeda flushes the tranquillisers prescribed by the doctor down the toilet. This final act is certainly not one of submission but rather of rebellion against the strategies of oppression used by institutions of authority (the psychiatrist and the husband) which stigmatize any individual who threatens to question or unsettle the status quo with the label 'mad'.

Madness which becomes the fate of middle-class women in Salwa Bakr's fiction can, from a different angle, be defined as the refusal of a human being to conform to pre-ordained cultural/ political/social/sexual roles. In 'Thirty-one beautiful green trees', Karima Fahmy reels under the harrowing pressures of a fast-decaying city. An inhabitant of the once beautiful city of Cairo, she bitterly mourns the brutal and systematic destruction of her city symbolized by the illogical massacre of thirty-one trees that shaded a familiar street. Her heightened awareness of the gravity of the matter alienates her from her world and turns her into a social misfit. Nevertheless, her reticence and isolation do not shield her from inevitable clashes with the forces of oppression that are implicitly to blame for the rapid deterioration of her world: she blows her top with her boss who is scandalized by her arrival at work without her brassière; she defies a manager at work who refuses to allow her to bring a red desk she had purchased instead of the grey one provided by the office; she is finally beaten up and arrested on election day for criticizing the hypocritical promises of political candidates. Back at home, she is dealt the final blow by her enslaved yet domineering mother who, having failed to socialize her rebellious daughter to accept the 'feminine' chains of bondage, commits her to an asylum. The end of the story is bitterly ironic: Karima's decision to comply, to submit to conventional social and gender roles, is epitomized by her attempt to cut off her tongue (an old threat of her mother's) which results in her complete ostracism from society.

Another of Salwa Bakr's characters, Farha, in 'Worms in the flower garden', actually loses her grip on reality when all the people in her world are metamorphosed in her eyes into worms. The nightmare of worms symbolically eating their way in a flower garden powerfully expresses Farha's disgust with her surroundings and her consequent alienation and estrangement. An unmarried, middle-class woman, she is mercilessly subjected to a complex string of conventions and customs that utterly entrap her and prevent her from saving her sanity. Hence, madness becomes 'the impasse confronting those whom cultural conditioning has deprived of the very means of protest or self-affirmation'.[17]

Visions of a mad world torment Nousa in 'The good old days'. Like the poetess in 'The world is out of joint', she is defeated by a strange world and turned into a passive, disillusioned individual. Nousa can hardly bring herself to get out of bed in the morning and, again like the poetess, does not even challenge the magazine editor when he makes a silly remark. Like Zeinat's lifestory in 'Zeinat at the President's funeral', Nousa's represents the disintegration of a personal dream which runs parallel to and coincides with the collapse of the national dream of an entire country. But, unlike Zeinat, Nousa surrenders to her fate without a fight. Similarly, after a frustrating experience, the poetess in 'The world is out of joint' goes home and decides that she needs a bath.

In the world of Salwa Bakr it is the illiterate, simple woman who has not been totally brainwashed by the popular media or by an oppressive educational system or by all the niceties of conventions and customs (sustained and propagated by the middle classes) who takes positive steps to change her life and her environment. In this way, Salwa Bakr manages to bring to the fore the suppressed discourse of women,[18] as Itidal Othman calls it, playing vital and effective roles in society, roles that destabilize the conventional, stereotypical patterns entrenched and popularized by the established discourse of the dominant culture.

In *The Golden Chariot Does Not Ascend to Heaven*, Salwa Bakr explores another course open to women for expressing their rebellion. The events of the novel take place in a women's prison inhabited by human beings more sinned against than sinners. Bakr depicts a rich and varied gallery of women prisoners, each telling a story of hardship and oppression. We meet the mother of al-Kheir, who chooses to save her son by taking the blame for his possessing narcotics. We sympathize with Aida, condemned to prison for killing her husband whereas she was only covering up for her brother, the real murderer. We also come across old Hanna, who murders her husband when, after a life of servitude and excessive sexual harassment, he threatens to throw her out in order to marry a younger woman. These women are condemned to prison because they are the traditional scapegoats of a society that values men more than women, boys more than girls. Old Hanna never contemplated the possibility of ending her marriage to a sexual maniac because she was brought up to believe it was her duty and obligation to please her husband and indulge his every whim. Her violent reaction erupts when she realizes that neither her old age nor her long history of compliance would plead for her and change her husband's decision to dispense with her. Old Hanna is the victim of a society that ostracizes women living outside wedlock. Her act of rebellion needs to be understood not only in the context of her private married life but also within the larger context of public values and conventions. It is noteworthy that Salwa Bakr does not single out man as the prime oppressor of woman. Her criticism is directed against the social norms and beliefs enforced by both men and women. In the case of Aida, it is the mother, not the father or brother, who ruthlessly sacrifices her daughter to save the more valuable son. Like Karima's mother, women can become fearsome agents of oppression once they accept the rules of an androcentric social order.

In *The Golden Chariot Does Not Ascend to Heaven*, Salwa Bakr also manages to transcend binary oppositions at the level of structure and style. The novel consists of a series of episodic portraits of women prisoners woven together by the point of view of a narrator, Aziza the Alexandrian. Convicted to life imprisonment for murdering her lover and stepfather, Aziza decides to escape the misery of a life in prison in a golden chariot that would ascend to heaven. She passes her time listening to the stories of other prisoners in order to select a group worthy of escorting her on her mythological journey. The development of the novel is not linear but cumulative: one experience is added on to another in a long sequence of episodes stitched together. The novel does not so much tell a story as project a live gallery of women in society. Bakr has not only carefully chosen her characters so as to represent different kinds of women, rich and poor, educated and uneducated, but has also managed to overcome the risk of stereotypical images through her description of minute details of their lives, thus bringing them very much alive.

Bakr's style also fuses the private and the public:

Ever since Aziza became aware of the tragic life of the Mother of Ragab, she changed her attitude towards her. She decided not to treat her as an old devil who never stopped fighting with everybody. She was indeed a trouble maker despite her thin body and her weak heart that was in danger of stopping any minute (prison doctors had said that she needed heart surgery, something that could never happen, of

course, because Mother of Ragab did not have a penny to her name
to pay a specialized surgeon who was bound to charge her a monu-
mental fee, and there was no hope going to state hospitals with limited
resources that could not possibly meet the demands of the long queues
of patients waiting at the door to receive medical treatment.)

Describing Aida, Bakr writes:

> Before her marriage, she got her diploma in commerce, a certificate of
> education that can only be described as a sly governmental trick to
> deceive generations of young people eager for an education that would
> give them access to good jobs.

In these excerpts, the writer blends public and private concerns in
the method of characterization. The reference to Mother of
Ragab's heart condition leads smoothly to a parenthetical comment about the corrupt medical system. Also, Aida's helplessness
in the face of social and parental oppression is aggravated by her
being one of many casualties of an education system that does not
ultimately empower individuals.

Bakr's style has invited criticism by those who failed to see the
point of blending social and private matters in the same sentence.
However, it is this style of writing that distinguishes Bakr's contribution making it unique and capable of expressing a woman's
point of view.

A Voice of Her Own

The evolution, articulation and dissemination of the suppressed
discourse of women, the ultimate goal of many capable and talented women writers, comes alive in the fiction of Salwa Bakr
because of her original style characterized by a magical fusion of
classical Arabic and Egyptian colloquial Arabic. In fact it is
practically impossible to write about Salwa Bakr without referring
to the special flavour of her style. Galal Amin is enchanted by her
revival of Egyptian colloquial expressions in the main course of
her narrative structure.[19] 'Popular proverbs and a linguistic tradition peculiar to the Egyptian scene' are dextrously blended in her
words, Gamal al-Ghitany remarks in his weekly column in al-
Akhbar.[20] And this same quality is described by Ferial Ghazoul as
balaghat al-ghalaba (the rhetoric of the have-nots).[21]

Salwa Bakr's language supersedes the dichotomy that is persist-
ently emphasized and exaggerated between colloquial and classical

Arabic. As she herself remarks, the majority of colloquialisms have roots in the classical language and only some words and phrases can be traced to foreign origins.[22] Therefore, she consciously employs what she describes as *al-amiyya al-fasiha* (classical colloquial language) in which colloquial words, phrases and structures with traceable Arabic roots are deftly woven into the sequence of her narrative. The ultimate effect of this style on the sensibility of the reader is one of moving and arresting sincerity. It is an effect which is unfortunately lost in translation due to the different relationship which exists in English between colloquial and standard language. Unlike colloquial English, colloquial Arabic is the language used by all classes of society, educated and uneducated alike, in their everyday life. Classical Arabic refers to the written language which is hardly ever used in speech except in formal addresses or on other official occasions. This dichotomy has some very serious implications for the creative writer, the most hazardous arising when he/she wishes to have their characters speak. The use of the formal classical Arabic in speech has an almost immediate distancing effect. Faced with this problem, writers have either resorted to colloquial Arabic in dialogue or have abided by the classical sequence throughout their narrative.

Not so for this writer. Liberated from binary thought that is only capable of approaching issues in an either/or fashion, Salwa Bakr blends the two variants of the language so beautifully as to create a new language that poignantly represents the point of view or the world view of her 'new' woman. On the level of narrative, Salwa Bakr touches upon the problems of the kind of language used in more than one story. Thus Zeinat questions the validity and sincerity of the formal stylized language used by Abdou, the grocer, in writing letters on her behalf. In her last letter to the President she insists on telling her story in her ordinary language, honestly and without recourse to formal stereotypes. Similarly, Fatma responds to Sophie's lecture on the necessity of birth control with the formal *wa huwa kathalik* (right you are). Whereas Sophie unconsciously reproduces the official, formal discourse in her conversation with her maid, Fatma's rejoinder is a conscious and deliberate mimicry of stylized clichés that are part of the repertoire of formal language. A voice of her own, both Salwa Bakr and her characters speak a new language that heralds and celebrates the discerning eye of the silenced Egyptian woman, not so silent any more.

Notes

1. Salwa Bakr has published four collections of short stories and two novels. *Zeinat at the President's funeral* (1986) was privately printed by the author. It was followed by *Atteya's Shrine* (Cairo: Dar al-Fikr lil-Dirasat wa'l-Nashr, 1986) and *About the Soul That Was Gradually Spirited Away* (Cairo: Misriyya lil Nashr wa'l-Tawzi, 1989). *The Golden Chariot Does Not Ascend to Heaven* (Cairo: Sina, 1991) was her first long novel to be followed by *The Description of the Nightingale* (Cairo: Sina, 1992) and then a collection of short stories *Rabbits* (Cairo: Sina, 1993). Bakr's work has been translated into many languages. Two collections of short stories have appeared in English: *Such a Beautiful Voice* translated by Hoda El Sadda (Cairo: General Egyptian Book Organization, 1992; reprinted by Kali, 1994) and *The Wiles of Men*, translated by Denys Johnson Davies (London: Quartet, 1992).

2. Elaine Showalter, *A Literature of Their Own* (London: Virago, 1978).

3. Elaine Showalter, 'Towards a feminist poetics' in Philip Rice and Patricia Waugh (eds), *Modern Literary Theory. A Reader* (London: Edward Arnold, 1989).

4. Rosalind Coward, 'Are women's novels feminist novels?' in Elaine Showalter (ed.), *The New Feminist Criticism: Essays on Women, Literature and Theory*, (New York: Pantheon Books, 1985).

5. Elaine Showalter, 'Feminist criticism in the wilderness', in *The New Feminist Criticism*, p. 249.

6. Hélène Cixous, 'The laugh of the Medusa' in Elaine Marks and Isabelle de Courtivron (eds), *New French Feminisms: An anthology* (Amherst: University of Massachusetts Press, 1980), pp. 259–60.

7. Ann Rosalind Jones, 'Writing the body: toward an understanding of l'écriture feminine' in *The New Feminist Criticism*, p. 369.

8. Julia Kristeva, 'Women's time' in Catherine Belsey and Jane Moore (eds), *The Feminist Reader: Essays in gender and the politics of literary criticism*, (London: Macmillan, 1989), p. 215.

9. Toril Moi, 'Feminist, female, feminine' in *The Feminist Reader*, p. 117.

10. Showalter, 'Feminist criticism in the wilderness', p. 266.

11. Suhair al-Qalamawy, Introduction, *Collection of Short Stories* (Cairo: Arab Women's Association, 1988).

12. Salwa Bakr, interview in *Nisf al-Dunia*, September 1991, pp. 54–5.

13. See Farouq Abdel Qader, 'The women of Salwa Bakr and *Her Golden Chariot*', *El Safir*, 21 April 1991.

14. Hélène Cixous, 'Sorties: out and out: Attacks/ways out/forays' in *The Feminist Reader*, p. 101.

15. Cixous, 'Sorties' p. 101.

16. Moi, 'Feminist, female, feminine', p. 125.

17. Shoshana Felman, 'Women and madness: the critical fallacy', in *The Feminist Reader*, p. 134.

18. Itidal Othman, 'Suppressed discourse in literature written by women', *al-Quds al-Arabi*, 17 April 1990.

19. Galal Amin, 'Salwa Bakr', *al-Hilal*, May 1991.

20. Gamal al-Ghitany, Review, *al-Akhbar*, 6 June 1990.

21. Ferial Ghazoul, 'Balaghat al-Ghalaba', *Contemporary Arab Thought an Women*, Proceedings of a conference held by the Arab Women's Solidarit Association (Cairo: Arab Women's Solidarity Publishing House, 1988).

22. Interview with translator.

8

Researching Gender in a Palestinian Camp: Political, Theoretical and Methodological Issues

Rosemary Sayigh

> The praxis of fieldwork, even in its most routinized and professionalized conception, never ceased to be an objective reflex of antagonistic political relations and, by the same token, a point of departure for a radical critique of anthropology.[1]

In the shadow of every completed piece of anthropological writing there lurks a history of false starts and unresolved problems that is suppressed by professional pressures to finish on time and produce a coherent account. This paper focuses on a particular fieldwork experience and tries to use it to explore dilemmas of researching gender in a Palestinian refugee camp in Lebanon.[2] It is written in response to the emergence of a number of distinct Middle Eastern feminist voices, by a feminist researcher who, though not Middle Eastern in origin, has partially become so through marriage and protracted residence. It is also prompted by the belief that discussion of problematic aspects of particular fieldwork experiences may be valuable in illuminating theoretical, political and methodological issues. The issues to be presented here are all linked to intersubjectivity, understood as the problem of the relationship between the researcher and the research community,[3] the politico-cultural worlds to which each belongs, and the ultimate purposes of the research project. Theoretical critiques such as those of Fabian, Asad, Dwyer and others have cast into relief the way that inequality between world regions, cultures and classes is created and reproduced by anthropology.[4] Intersubjectivity differs radically from the classical anthropological concept of rapport in that it is not a technique of entry to a research milieu, nor of establishing relationships through which data may be extracted, but rather is a concept that calls into question all stages of research, from conception to writing up. It focuses critical attention not on findings, as in the empiricist tradition, nor on textuality, as in some post-modern approaches, but on the theory and politics of the representation of 'other' cultures, and on the meaning and consequences of research for the researched. Eliciting research community assent to particular research topics would be one way of realizing intersubjectivity, but theorists like Dwyer have also underlined the vulnerability of the researcher: her/his identity and subjectivity cannot be abstracted from the research process.

Statements of researcher positionality have become a rite of introduction. Nonetheless, there are complex consequences that need to be explored, for example the effect on respondents' speech and behaviour of their perceptions of the researcher's identity and purposes. Different components of the researcher's identity— ethnic origins, gender, class, marital/parental status, age, political orientations—are brought into play in the field, opening up certain experiences and understandings, closing off others. The researcher enters the field with particular aims and interests that often change through the fieldwork experience: initial ideas of the research community are likely to be revised, as well as the formulation of the research project. Attention to positionality also raises the question of cultural perspectives and hybridity. As the notion of the ethnographer as detached, culturally neutral, 'scientific' observer is eroded, space is created for consideration of the way in which the researcher's origins and background shape field experiences and interpretations.[5] Thus a second aim of this chapter is to question the effects of prolonged exposure to a specific culture (in my case, that of Palestinian exiles in Lebanon). While culturally enriching, hybridity perhaps induces a half-conscious adoption of the research community's ethos; and this, while enhancing rapport, may block off certain questions and lines of enquiry.

While this paper follows a chronological rather than analytic sequence, I have focused the narrative around three main problems, the choice of gender as a topic of enquiry, women's life histories as a form of observation, and the selection of respondents. All three have theoretical, political and methodological implications and all three link back to the principle of intersubjectivity. In the case of choice of the research topic, it is the principle of the research community's assent that is invoked: how could the researcher's concern with gender be legitimized to a community undergoing national crisis and military siege? The decision to record women's life stories appeared to guarantee certain kinds of autonomy: did historical, social and cultural factors place constraints on this autonomy? The third problem, that of choice of women narrators, also raises issues of intersubjectivity: whose schema of representation should prevail, the researcher's or the research community's?

The Politics of Gender as a Research Topic

Kandiyoti argues persuasively that feminists working in the Middle East should not be inhibited from researching gender from fear of exhibiting Western ethnocentrism.[6] I entered the field with an initial interest in studying women's lives but I was equally strongly convinced that research among oppressed and marginal collectivities should be responsive to their definitions of their situation. Both concerns have well-established foundations in recent critical anthropological theory. Though not intrinsically antithetical, they formed a source of inner conflict during fieldwork, especially in the protracted period of entry after 1982, when I was trying out different research approaches in a community struggling to survive war and political oppression. However convinced I was of the centrality of gender hierarchy to all forms of inequality, global and local, I also felt the weight of two kinds of objection to carrying out feminist ethnography in a Palestinian camp. On the epistemological level, there were the objections raised by Mohanty, Lazreg and others, which 'locate' feminist theory as a product of Western experience and discourse, insufficiently inflected to accommodate other realities.[7] In this perspective, feminist ethnography may be seen as what Asad calls a 'strong language', through which Western cultural frameworks are imposed, through research questions and 'cultural translation', on non-Western cultures and reality.[8] A second kind of objection lay in the historical experience and contemporary situation of Palestinian exiles in Lebanon which appeared to make gender as a research topic suspect or irrelevant. I shall briefly attempt to outline in what ways this was so.

Empirically speaking, Palestinian camp communities offer fertile milieus for the study of gender because of the sharpness of the contradictions they contain and the articulate way in which these are voiced. Camps have been exposed to multiple sources and types of pressure that have tended to modify pre-1948 gender ideology and practice—UNRWA schooling, the employment of women, the Lebanese environment, secondary migration and, most importantly, mobilization in the Resistance movement. At the same time, because camps attempted to preserve pre-1948 relations of kinship and locality, they formed cultural contexts that expressly stood against changes in gender relations. Indeed, as a general reaction to exile, gender became articulated and politicized as it had not been in Palestine, transformed into a central element in popular resistance to culture loss and alienation. When people of the camps expressed pride in having preserved 'our customs and traditions', it was precisely rules about gender relations that they meant. Women, just like men or village and family notables, shared in this pride which most saw as necessary protection for themselves and the community, surrounded by an alien dominant society.[9] As a specifically Palestinian identity was formed in the camps out of the experience of exile in Lebanon, it was articulated largely in terms of fidelity to origins. Palestinian women were viewed by men and women as harder working, stricter about honour, and better mothers than Lebanese women; and such perceptions formed a central element in Palestinian self-differentiation from the Lebanese.

Chatterjee alerts us to another factor politicizing gender: the need of communities subjected to state oppression to protect an 'inner domain' from penetration.[10] This was true in a very literal sense of Palestinian camps in the 1960s, the period of their control by the Army Intelligence Bureau. As a humiliating expression of their knowledge and power, the authorities used to tell camp people: 'We know when any man sleeps with his wife.' Knowledge about personal relationships was used by the authorities to persecute activists and recruit informers. Fear of state intrusion was so pronounced among camp dwellers that internal acts of violence, for example 'honour' crimes against women, were concealed with the complicity of the whole community. The habit of self-protection and dissimulation inculcated by oppression radiated inwards from the community to individual families who also felt the necessity to guard their 'inner domain' from the scrutiny of others, whether neighbours, state agents or UNRWA officials.

With the arrival of the Resistance movement, from 1969, there developed a far more dynamic, indigenous challenge to constraints on women than those brought about as a result of exile.[11] Women as well as men were recruited into the movement's multiple

structures, civilian and military. Paid employment for women expanded, especially between 1976 and 1982, as the PLO developed
a proto-state apparatus, with administrative, social and economic
sectors. But nationalist discourse blocked discussion of the 'woman
question' by defining it as 'secondary', by emphasizing 'organic
unity' between the national and women's movements, and by
calling on women to liberate themselves through joining the
national struggle. Such slogans made it difficult for women to
discuss publically problems they encountered as women in the
movement.[12] Activist women were divided by their Resistance
affiliations, which directed their consciousness and work into par-
tisan channels and weakened the General Union of Palestinian
Women (GUPW), the structure best suited for work among women
in camps.

An experience of my own, before 1982, with the GUPW points
to problems of doing research about women even within the
framework of an indigenous women's movement. I tried to interest
the GUPW's Lebanon Branch in a collaborative research project
on conditions of women in the camps. That this attempt failed
underlines the 'cultural politics' of gender research and the critical
nature of the researcher's identity. As a Western woman, I was
likely to be more feminist than nationalist, an orientation that
might threaten the GUPW's ethos. My lack of Resistance group
affiliation formed a second, perhaps more threatening kind of
'difference'. Although marriage to a Palestinian made me a quasi-
'insider', it required association with one of the Resistance groups
to make me fully a member, like them classifiable and accountable
within the Resistance 'family'. Nationalist women may also have
feared that a study of women in the camps would reflect negatively
on the movement.

At the level of the camps, in spite of deep support for the
national movement, there were many kinds of resistance to change
in gender ideology and practice, resistances that coexisted with
actual instances of pragmatic change. By recruiting their sons and
daughters, the Resistance movement threatened age and gender
hierarchies through which families controlled junior members. The
close relation between family status and the reputation of its female
members made young unmarried women a focal point of conflict
between the Resistance and camp families, as well as within
families themselves. Such conflict could arise over many issues,
from attending political meetings, joining a Resistance group to

marrying a 'stranger'; and attempting to mediate offered women cadres a useful entry point through which to politicize camp families.

After 1982, with the evacuation of the PLO and the reinstallation of Lebanese Army authority, political, economic and ideological conditions in the camps changed radically. On one level, crisis brought out camp women's agency and activism and made it more visible. With men largely absent—evacuated, in prison, in hiding, disabled or dead—women took on multiple tasks, repairing war-damaged homes, demonstrating, carrying messages and money between the war-zones, trying to get prisoners released, directing social institutions and distributing supplies.[13] Yet in the aftermath of 1982, change in women's clothing became visible, with the jeans and bare heads associated with the Resistance movement given up in favour of long-sleeved, long-skirted dresses and head-coverings. Less visibly, many practices declared to have ended during the Resistance period, such as coercive marriage of daughters at very early ages, reappeared.

Although this contrast between pre- and post-1982 conditions offered a feminist ethnographer an unusual and fertile opening for research, I remained mired for several years in trying to find a formulation that would reconcile a dual concern with gender and intersubjectivity. What way of researching gender would respond to the new, more crisis-ridden situation of camp communities, incorporating their concerns as well as mine? Another aspect of my identity, my unemployed-housewife status, gave me several years to work through this dilemma, a trial period seldom available to the professional anthropologist.

Fieldwork in Crisis

For the outsider, entry to Shateela camp before and after 1982 were as different as life had become for the camp's people, with different monitoring authorities to pass through, and different attributions of identity and purpose from those inside the camp. My foreign identity and my age helped protect me from interrogation by Lebanese Army units surrounding the camp and patrolling its interior since they associated these characteristics with social work. But entry into the research community was another story, impeded by the climate of fear created by army arrests and militia kidnappings. Female foreign social workers were not necessarily harmless: they could be spies for any of a number of hostile forces. It was a time when even neighbours might turn out to be informers and when people returned to habits of reserve and self-concealment bred by long struggle against oppression. An often quoted saying at that time was '*hayt al-hayt*', translatable as 'keep your head down'.

An even greater difficulty was to imagine research that could be responsive to such conditions. While conscience can be eased by the many kinds of actions anthropologists undertake when working in communities in crisis—reporting human rights violations, passing on information about aid or jobs—such actions do not solve the theoretical and political problem of choice of research topic. As the camp Popular Committee dissolved itself and Resistance cadres returned to semi-clandestinity, there was no longer any representative body with which to negotiate my presence and purposes.

At the beginning I resorted to the UNRWA clinic as a base inside the camp, accompanying the Staff Nurse on home visits to pregnant women and mothers of underweight babies. Such an association posed limitations, however, so I renewed pre-1982 ties with a particular Shateela family, spending whole days with them and often sleeping overnight. One of the questions that may be put to this classic way of doing fieldwork is that it skirts the necessity of open presentation of the researcher's intentions to the community at large. As the adopted household transforms the researcher, first into a welcome visitor, then protégé, then quasi-member, initial questions about her/his purposes are forgotten. Identification with a particular household confers legitimacy and ease of entry to other households. In a sense, *not* asking about intentions is a sign of friendship; to ask would show distance and suspicion.[14]

Political conditions after 1982 also brought into sharp relief anthropology's reliance on the question as an elementary tool of research, and underlined the awkward relationship between questions and interrogations. I discovered there were no innocent questions; even questions I put to people about the past (which I naively hoped would be 'safe') elicited such responses as 'Why do you want to know?' It was almost as difficult to question Umm Khaled,[15] my friend and sponsor, about the people she took me to visit. Although Umm Khaled trusted me politically, discretion reduced her responses to my questions to a minimum, for example 'They're friends', or 'They're very good people'. Thus, for the first two years of fieldwork I knew people's faces, and where they lived, but nothing else about them. To people who asked Umm Khaled who I was and what I was doing she always replied, 'She's married to a Palestinian, and she sympathizes with us.' The identity of 'sympathizer' was an acceptable one since Shateela people were used to receiving visits from pro-Palestinian delegations. But the difference between pre- and post-1982 political conditions is underlined by the ways Peteet was introduced in Shateela before 1982 as 'researcher', 'comrade' and 'sister'.[16] Though Umm Khaled sustained her pre-1982 visiting network, which included elements of her husband's Resistance group, all political references were carefully edited out. This difficulty of asking questions highlighted for me how taken-for-granted questioning is as a tool in social science practice, and how laden with assumptions about researcher-researched hierarchy.

Uneasiness with questions was deepened by several fieldwork experiences. The first occurred when another researcher conducted a questionnaire with Abu Khaled in my presence. The subject of the questionnaire was parental attitudes towards daughters, and one of the questions was, 'Would you force your daughter to marry a man she doesn't want?' Abu Khaled, who belonged to one of the progressive Resistance groups, answered emphatically that he would not. Yet it was just at this time that he had agreed to a request for one of his daughters in marriage and, though she had given her assent, her unhappiness about it was visible. This incident was revealing on several levels. First, of course, it illustrated the unreliability of questionnaires. Second, it pointed not only to the way that the researcher's identity influences responses, but also to the complex nature of identity, composed of elements that participants perceive differently depending on their own positionality. That this researcher was Palestinian, possibly a member of the same Resistance group as his, doubtless encouraged Abu Khaled to respond to the questionnaire in the first place. His response to the question about daughters may have been influenced by shared Resistance group affiliation, and perhaps also by the fact that the researcher was a woman. But, though Palestinian, she was still an 'outsider' to the camp, someone to whom Abu Khaled felt no obligation to expose his dilemmas as father and as party member.

On another level, this incident was the first of several that made me aware of the problems for a researcher of becoming, but not fully being, an 'insider'. I felt inhibited by the sensitivity of the topic from questioning Abu Khaled about the discrepancy between his professed convictions and his actual behaviour, especially since this would be to implicitly accuse him of lying. A real 'insider'— family member, neighbour, or male friend—would certainly have challenged him but, though in some respects more of an 'insider' than the researcher administering the questionnaire, I did not feel sufficiently an 'insider' to probe the motives of someone who sponsored my presence in the camp. Then and later the status of 'guest' seemed to impose a set of obligations and constraints that were almost impossible to reconcile with the aims of research. If building rapport between researcher and respondent is only a means of entry, a mere part of the technology of ethnographic research, is it not a form of deceit? And if the researcher's developing identity as guest and friend is genuine, is it compatible with probing questions and possibly damaging accounts?

This phase of fieldwork was brought violently to an end by the Amal militia attack of May/June 1985, during which Umm Khaled's home was destroyed, forcing her to move to Sidon with the children. The battles that lasted on and off from 1985 to mid-1988 scattered most Shateela people outside the camp. A few families remained inside, but access was barred by Syrian and Fateh-dissident checkpoints; entry was almost impossible for non-residents, and informers inside were likely to report on all contacts. This effectively ended the possibility of participant observation, and forced me to find alternative ways of continuing fieldwork. I began to visit women in *muhajareen* (war-displaced) centres, sometimes recording their histories of work, earnings, relationships and management of household economies: a strategy based on a feminist reading of Engels. Respondents were women who already knew me as 'friend of Umm Khaled'. Problematic aspects of this project arose not so much from gaining the assent of the researched, for visits gave women a welcome break in days spent struggling with the hardships of *muhajareen* existence. Rather they arose, first, from the question of the importance of women's earnings within a context of national crisis: could these be separated from other aspects of crisis such as political activities or the intensification of domestic burdens? There was also an ethical problem in asking about earnings and income when no material benefits were likely to result.

It was during this phase, while trying to use visits as a method of research, that I began realize how people of the camps feel about visits: what visits mean and how they should be conducted, what topics of conversation are preferred and what topics should be avoided. Such awareness increased the tension between my purposes as researcher and my identity as 'friend'. Often I seemed to be asking people questions that recalled tragic memories. Delicately, an older woman whose home had been shattered, when I asked about her life before moving to Shateela, told me the saying *al-gham bighum* ('sad things make people sad'). Another whom I asked about her work as a nurse in the 1950s replied: 'So many (bad) things have happened since then, I can't remember those days. It makes my head ache.' Here again my question appeared as *gheir marghoub* (a description often used of behaviour that is disliked, ill-advised). Subjects brought up during visits, I was made to feel, should be as different as possible from 'real life': entertaining, amusing, possibly informative and edifying, but never close to the suffering of anyone present. Smuggling research questions into ordinary conversations became harder as I sensed the degree to which visits should express friendship and real concern for the other person's well-being.

Not asking questions seemed deeply ingrained in camp customs. A Shateela man whom I had asked why his parents had left the camp where most of the people of their village lived told me, 'I never dug it up.' The implication that 'digging things up' is at best impolite, at worst suspect, was reinforced by his quotation of a proverb where 'to dig' (*yuhfur*), is synonymous with 'creating calamity'. How important 'not asking' is to the practice of good relations is shown by another anecdote. Umm Subhi was telling me about her friend and neighbour whose husband had just died: 'She has different mourning customs because she's from a Bedouin family whereas he was a villager.' My curiosity aroused by this breach of custom, I asked her 'How did they come to marry?' Umm Subhi replied, 'I never asked.' She went on to explain: 'I don't ask such questions. Even if she's a friend she might begin to wonder "Why is she asking me this?".'

Ethnographers often feel they have to choose between pursuit of predetermined questions, and intervening as little as possible in order to preserve a state of 'naturalness'. Joseph describes how she found herself using two different methods, one learnt in graduate school—'male', active, systematic—the other based in her family upbringing as an Arab woman—'female', passive, informal and indirect—and notes how much information a researcher unconsciously assimilates through friendship.[17] Abu-Lughod also reports experiencing conflict early in her fieldwork between what she felt she should be doing as ethnographer— 'going from door to door, meeting everyone in the vicinity, conducting surveys'— and the behaviour necessitated by her position as 'dutiful daughter'.[18] Though such internal tensions may be painful, and certainly slow down the processes of research, they are valuable in pressing the ethnographer to find a way to integrate her/his identities as 'researcher' and 'friend' rather than experience them as separate and hierarchized. Such integration has theoretical as well as moral implications, abolishing illusions of objectivity and of non-relationship with the research community, since whether or not the researcher adopts an advocacy stance, she/he cannot help but be a presence, with particular effects on and for members as a 'specialist' who will interpret them to the world.[19]

Further battles and displacement in 1988 made consultation about the purposes of my research even more unfeasible, yet the threat to the existence and future of the community, through its sheer magnitude, pointed to a way of solving the problem of intersubjectivity. From their beginnings, camps in Lebanon have been subject to authoritarian control, attack and coercive change. At the same time they have been arenas of complex processes of resistance and adaptation. Yet this rich historical experience has gone mainly unrecorded. I felt that to record Shateela peoples' recollections of the past in this moment of extremity was a way of responding to their need to be written into history, a way that would link the worlds represented by researcher and researched, and give the researcher a local community role as scribe. From the beginning this work evoked enthusiasm and collaboration, even though political conditions prevented it from being fully appropriated by the research community. The keeping of siege diaries and recordings with old people done by others at this time was another sign of a common mood. At this point in my fieldwork, history appeared as a bridge between my interests as researcher and those of the research community.

In feminism, too, the concept of history has had multiple uses, in theorizing and research as well as in consciousness-raising and mobilization. Particularly in the case of anti-colonial struggles, the discrepancy between women's participation and their marginalization in national politics and histories has fuelled specific forms of feminism that often take the form of attempts to reconstitute a 'female collective memory'.[20] Reflection on specificities of the Palestinian case suggested that there were at least as many women's histories as there were state boundaries dividing the diaspora and class boundaries among the Palestinian people. Recording with women in a single camp in one host regime would have obvious limitations. Yet, given the richness of historical experience and articulateness of women in camp communities in Lebanon, I was convinced that such a project would have value as a national and women's archive.

The Life-Story:
Imposed or Autonomous Form?

Anthropologists in particular have raised a number of questions about the life-story as a medium for capturing collective history by problematizing the 'typicality' of speakers and reliability of memory,[21] highlighting the redundancy of life-stories and their artificiality as a product of the demand of the anthropologist,[22] and querying the assumptions of a coherent 'self' which they impose.[23] Abu-Lughod's objection that the 'life-story may contribute to a sense of the person at its centre as an isolated individual' arises from living with Bedouin women who, she notes, do not live or think of themselves in this way.[24] However, the theoretical introduction given by Passerini to her use of life-stories for her study of Italian workers' memories of Fascism meets many of these objections.[25] Passerini evokes the 'self' not as a psychodynamic entity but as 'revealing cultural attitudes, visions of the world and interpretations of history'.[26] For her, subjectivity is an arena in which ideological and political struggles are played out, and in which historically transmitted elements of popular culture are displayed. Though care is needed in eliciting and interpreting life stories not to over-individualize them, these notions are as relevant for ethnographers working in 'Third World' milieus as for European historians.

Recording women's life-stories also seemed to offer a solution to the problem of research community assent, since respondents appeared free to record or refuse to do so. More importantly, they were free to choose what to say and what to omit. The life-story as method also removes intrusive researcher questions, 'giving the floor' to the life-story teller. With experience and reflection, however, problems with the life-story emerged. It became clear first, that the autonomy of the life-story narrator is limited by the situation of the collectivity. Individual Shateela women could (and some did) refuse my invitations to record but this was the limit of their power—there was no collective forum in which they could question the project, or modify it, or suggest speakers, or join in carrying it out. Further, the fact that most of the women I invited to record agreed to do so was open to interpretations which cast doubt on their real autonomy. For example, assent could be attributed to a history of class and national oppression and to present insecurity: 'studying down' is less likely to meet with non-co-operation than 'studying up'.[27] It could also be linked to habits of nationalist testimony encouraged by the Resistance movement. Established relations of visiting might also have made refusal embarrassing. Further, the women who recorded had no control over the eventual uses to which their life-stories would be put, taking their powerlessness in this regard so much for granted that most did not even ask. The significance of this point was brought home to me when a life-story teller whom I was reassuring that her words would remain confidential answered that, on the contrary, she wanted the world to know her story.

It became clear, also, that consent to being recorded sometimes hid a real disinclination that could not be expressed through outright refusal. The most suggestive evidence comes from the very sketchy stories that some subjects gave me, bare skeletons of displacement and loss. Two examples point to reasons women might have for saying little even after having consented to speak. One is Umm Mahmoud. When I first visited her she expressed reluctance to record a life that had been 'nothing but tragedy'. Eventually, however, she consented because I came with a recommendation from her son. She gave a very brief narrative consisting mainly of disasters that had happened to the Palestinian people and to her own family. But during a later visit she described an episode of detention in Damascus, when she was held for several days and extensively interrogated. The interrogators had demanded that she tell them 'everything about my life, without leaving out anything'. The parallel between this episode and my own request for her life-story was clear, and helped to explain the brevity of her narrative. This was a dismaying discovery, underlying the point made by the Popular Memory Group, in their critique of conventional oral history practice, that merely to speak to a subordinate changes nothing about her/his situation.

Another field experience also points to problematic aspects of the life-story. I met Umm Nader by chance in a torrential rain-storm and we struck up a friendship immediately, drying our shoes out in her 'squat' in the ruined American Embassy. In this first meeting she talked so easily about herself that I asked straightaway if she would let me record her life-story. She agreed. But when it took place a few days later, the recording consisted of little more than a list of the homes from which she had been displaced, and of sons who had been imprisoned or killed. Perhaps she sensed the disappointment I tried to hide because she added, 'This isn't the first time I've told my story. We've met so many delegations, and so many journalists, and talked to them, and nothing has ever come out of it.' In Umm Nader's case as in Umm Mahmoud's, I felt that pressing them to recall lives so full of pain and loss was close to torture. I could offer little in return for their testimonials while my relative immunity from such painful experi-ences appeared only to deepen 'difference' between us. Though a researcher engaged in 'advocacy anthropology' hopes that know-ledge of the lives of the oppressed can make a political difference, this cannot be guaranteed to those who give testimony.

In the introduction to her book on Brazilian women's life-stories, Patai raises the issue of the particular intimacy and one-sidedness of the life-story: 'A woman telling her life-story is in a sense offering up her self for her own and her listener's scrutiny.'[28] Abu-Lughod makes a related point, though with a different em-phasis: 'I was asking them to be honest so that I could learn what their lives were like, but at the same time I was unwilling to reveal much about myself.'[29] Though I aimed at openness about my own life while in the field, answering questions put to me by members of the research community, boundaries of culture and class limited the degree of reciprocity in such self-disclosure. Camp women's uses for snippets of information I offered could not be compared with my uses of their lives: a dissertation, perhaps a book. It is noticeable that Patai, after discussing the ethical problems of life-story collection among low-income women, jumps over solutions to the excitement of life-story recording, 'the sheer pleasure of listening to a person weave a tale'.[30] But such listening, however important, changes little in life-story givers' lives unless incorporated into a larger, collectively directed project such as the one among Puerto Rican women in New York described by Benmayor.[31]

From my own perspective as researcher, the choice of life-stories as a form of data also posed problems. On the one hand, national crisis gave many women an authentic motive for recording their life-stories, a motive that was simultaneously personal and collective. The life-story form, by allowing them to opt for a purely national narrative, partially satisfied the demands of inter-subjectivity. But I feared that the national crisis and nationalistic discourse would so dominate what respondents would remember and recount that their experiences of gender and sexuality would be eliminated. This was especially likely as, in an attempt to make them 'natural', I recorded all but two of the life-stories in public, in the presence of family and friends, a decision that seemed bound to enhance their nationalism and to repress gender issues.[32]

I also feared that the conventions of nationalist ideology would 'mould' the life-stories, and turn them into exemplars of credos such as that the Resistance movement had liberated women.[33] I even considered using the life-stories as a first stage towards later questions about gender and sexuality. But on reflection this seemed like an unspoken bargain along the lines of 'I'll record your nation-alism if in exchange you tell me about gender relations.' Further, I realised that in a milieu where references to gender and sexuality are either repressed or expressed indirectly, one would have to be a native speaker to manage such questions properly.

Later, as I listened to the life-stories, it became evident that I had exaggerated the degree to which nationalism would displace, suppress or propagandize gender issues. Certainly, the chronology of the Palestinian national crisis structured narration in most of the life-stories, while nationalist feelings pervaded them. But gender was multiply present, a starting point with consequences that were both inescapable and malleable. Gender was imprinted upon women's nationalism and national crisis had shaped their living of gender. Even sexuality, a potentially taboo area, was not as strictly edited out as I had feared it would be. In two of the life-stories it formed the central node around which narration re-volved. In others it was referred to obliquely; and, as I ought to have known, elisions of references to sexuality offer their own insights. Perhaps the hardships experienced by Palestinians in Lebanon since the departure of the PLO had eroded the hegemony of nationalist discourse. In any case, my dilemma was solved by the honesty and richness of camp women's stories.

Interviewing Palestinian women in very different political

conditions, during the Intifada in the Occupied Territories, Gluck writes perceptively of the tensions between 'advocacy oral history' and her research interest in gender: 'Could I bring my usual critical interviewing skills to bear? Could I...avoid becoming a mere conduit for political platforms?'[34] Few others of the many recent writers about Palestinian women have confronted so perspicaciously the problem that nationalism may colour the perceptions and reports of the 'sex-gender system' of *both respondents and researchers*. The advantage of life-stories in comparison with interviews is that the self-generated narrative leaves women freer to express and suppress the 'sex-gender system' in their own ways. Whereas face-to-face interviews are likely to activate a nationalist narrative, especially if the interviewer is Western, the form and flow of a life-story allows other determinants, for example culture, class and generation, to influence the way gender and sexuality are dealt with.

The question of nationalism *vis-à-vis* gender arises again in later stages of research, in interpretation and writing up. There are both political and theoretical reasons why the researcher's observations should be taken back to the field before publication. The account given by Mbilinyi of life-story recording with an older, rural woman lay-preacher in Tanzania illustrates this point well.[35] Though both researcher and life-story giver shared Tanzanian nationality, differences of generation, class and culture caused Mbilinyi to fail to perceive an indigenous form of feminism practised by older Tanzanian women in rural areas. Only collaborative research and checking back allowed this misrepresentation to be corrected. My interpretations of Palestinian camp women's life-stories would certainly have benefited from such checking back; but this was impeded, except in a few cases, by political conditions and the large size of the sample (twenty cases), chosen to demonstrate heterogeneity and obtain historical depth. Discussions I could not have with the life-story tellers were partially compensated for, however, by the comments of colleagues who helped with translation.

These colleagues were young Palestinian women from milieus close to the camps, who became part of the research project in unanticipated ways. As we listened to the tapes together, their comments offered other views distinct from my own and that of the life-story tellers. Particular episodes often sparked them into telling fragments of their own lives, in confirmation or contrast.

Life-story tellers were told about this collaborative listening, which could have been disturbing, especially in one case where narrator and translator-colleague knew each other. No one objected, perhaps because of the public character of the recording sessions, or because people at that time had more serious worries.

In terms of writing up, the issue in my case was not so much the one raised by Abu-Lughod on the ethics of conveying intimate personal data into the public realm.[36] Most of the women who told their life-stories were consciously speaking through me to 'the world'. Indeed this is what legitimized their speaking at all, and several of them underlined this public purpose by including the hope that people outside would understand the justice of the Palestinian cause (thereby creating a new dilemma since, if I failed to publicize their message, I would be breaking the implicit condition upon which they offered their stories). The issue was rather that, by using their life-stories to analyse the relationship between nationalism and gender, I was going beyond their intentions. They had spoken to me primarily as Palestinians, and as if I would convey their speech to the world *in its totality*. But I had listened to them primarily as women, and had subjected their words to my own purposes as feminist ethnographer.

The Question of Representation, or Who Should Speak ?

The selection of 'informants' from the research community is always a question with theoretical and political implications, with links to the principle of intersubjectivity. On a theoretical level, words turned into text form part of the eventual representation of the research community; *whose* words must shape and colour the picture? Ignoring indigenous self-knowledge, as in all versions of structural anthropology, is constitutive of allochrony and 'difference'. The question of who speaks is even more central when, as in life-story recording, interpretation is almost wholly based on elicited speech rather than on observation of 'natural' interaction. As for political aspects, especially in crisis communities, the selection of speakers is doubly politicized, since crisis both intensifies the need of a collectivity to represent itself to others *and* internal struggles over who should speak for the collectivity and what they should say. To see this question as merely one of 'sampling' and as a purely methodological problem, is to impose social science criteria, demographic or social structural, over the self-knowledge and desires of the research community. To represent internal differences adequately requires an intersubjective understanding of what these are.

In order to locate potential life-story tellers, I needed to discover how the research community categorizes women. At the same time I felt constrained by a prior research commitment mentioned earlier, namely demonstrating the heterogeneity of women in even a small milieu (in opposition to the Orientalist assumptions of their homogeneity), and discovering historical change in relation to nationalism and gender, both of which dictated a rather large number of speakers. A large sample also allowed the inclusion of varieties of political affiliations and types of activism, as well as of work outside the home. I was also constrained by perceptions accumulated in the field and by the boundaries of my network. It is on two kinds of tension between these researcher perspectives and those of the research community with respect to the choice of speakers that this section focuses.

The first stage of enquiry (with a male colleague) pointed to a revealing absence of variety or, put differently, the predominance of a single type: *al-mar'a al-baitiyya* (the housewifely woman) further described in terms such as *ma btitla wa la btinzal* ('she doesn't come and go') or *al-bait wa bass* ('the home and nothing else'). My colleague also spoke of the basic distinction *al-mar'a* (woman, wife) and *al-bint* (girl or virgin), based on sexual experience, as well as the highly varied terms denoting marital and life-cycle statuses. Women colleagues used these too but added others, for example *mnazemi* or *mhazabi* ('organized', member of a Resistance group), *mar't al-shaheed* and *umm al-shaheed* (respectively wife and mother of the martyr, i.e. a man killed in the national struggle).

Inquiry also revealed a category of woman denoted as *(q)awiyya* (strong). This term has ambivalent resonance: it is used positively in nationalist discourse to describe women who are active in the movement and who can bear hardship and loss. But used by ordinary people (less educated, less politicized, older), it can have an undertone of criticism, as if strong women are a symptom of a deplorable situation. Depending on the tone of voice, a woman described as '*(q)awiyya*' may be either a model of patriotism or someone who dominates or manipulates others for personal ends. Another, rarely used categorization is *mistarjali*, describing women who are man-like (from *rajul*, man) in being economically independent, someone who, because of her earning power or control over household income, dominates her husband or, if a widow, cuts herself from male kinsfolk. It is probable that conditions of exile have encouraged the phenomenon of the *mistarjali* women, a consideration that made me eager to record with one. It became evident, however, that such women are disapproved of because of the way they invert conventional gender hierarchy and flout norms of decorum. There had been such a woman in Shateela before 1982, but she had left with the Resistance in 1982. Though she had been celebrated by the Resistance movement, Shateela people said she was not admired by them. An older woman remarked, 'We loved her because she lost a son, not because she was patriotic.' The difficulty I had in finding such a *mistarjali* woman to record with suggests that economic independence may strain their ties with kin and local community.

Asked to suggest women to be recorded, people mostly proposed political activists, mothers or wives of martyrs, or directors of social institutions—strong, politicized, articulate women. While the desire of a crisis community to be represented by people of this type is understandable, my own desire was for a sample that would include 'ordinary' women, the kind that militants before 1982 used to describe as 'far from the Revolution'. Had I been collaborating with GUPW or Resistance activists this would probably have been an issue of dispute. Activist women might also have argued that *all* Resistance groups should be represented, according to PLO prescriptions, and perhaps also that 'responsibles' should be chosen to speak rather than ordinary members, moves that would (from my point of view) overburden the sample with political women. Problematic aspects of the interaction between nationalism and gender were not likely to be illuminated by the life-stories of women leaders. I was made aware after recording with a junior, somewhat 'feminist' cadre from one of the smaller Resistance groups, that this choice was not approved of by a GUPW local leader.

Another dilemma of selection, whether to try to include women viewed by the research community as deviant, raised a different aspect of intersubjectivity. Though friends in Shateela might speak about prostitution in general terms, it would be hard for them to name specific cases from the local community; and I was sure they would refuse to guide me if I had attempted to meet anyone accused of being 'loose'. The moral and social importance of the boundary between controlled and uncontrolled sexuality for people of the camps means that it cannot lightly be crossed. Too much curiosity about deviance on my part would have appeared intrusive and suspect. Faced with a choice between including deviant women and endangering (as it seemed) my project, I yielded to my understanding of community values.[37] It was only later, in post-fieldwork reflection, that I asked myself why had I so easily abandoned the idea of recording deviance. What considerations had really been at stake? Was I afraid of losing the network I had built up over several years in the field? Had I through long association adopted what I took to be the research community's gender ethos, thus attributing to it an artificial definiteness and permanence? Where did I now stand on this issue myself? Was it one of 'sampling' or of human rights? Here again, public discussion of this question would have been a useful step, possibly bringing out different views, and counteracting the tendency of empirical research to reproduce existing knowledge.

Conclusion

I have written this paper as a narrative that recapitulates a particular fieldwork experience and teases out political, theoretical and methodological problems that were elided from the first account. It is a narrative that interweaves three histories; that of Shateela camp in the 1980s, my own as researcher, and that of the research project, itself the product of interaction between camp community and researcher. The particularity of these histories does not make them incapable of illustrating some general problems in anthropology: crisis heightens problems of entry, reciprocity, purpose, and representation but also makes their political and theoretical implications more sharply revealing. Inner conflicts between concern with gender and a stance of advocacy towards the rights of Palestinian people illustrate the essential fallacy underlying the neutral, observer stance adumbrated by classical anthropology.

Notes

I should like to thank Deniz Kandiyoti and Suad Joseph for helpful comments on the first draft of this paper; also Tim Niblock and Norman O'Neill, my thesis examiners, for their careful reading of my thesis; and

Talal Asad, Michael Hitchcock and Ann Hunt for encouraging me to the finish line.

Notes

1. Johannes Fabian, *Time and the Other* (New Jersey, 1983), p. 149.

2. This work was presented as a doctoral dissertation in the Department of Sociology and Anthropology, the University of Hull, 1994, under the title 'Palestinian camp women's narratives of exile: self, gender, national crisis'.

3. I use this term throughout without presumptions of external boundaries or internal homogeneity, to refer to local, national or other forms of collectivity to which the people I am writing about feel they belong.

4. Fabian, *Time and the Other*; Talal Asad, 'The concept of cultural translation in British social anthropology' in James Clifford and George Marcus (eds), *Writing Culture* (Berkeley: University of California Press, 1986); Kevin Dwyer, *Moroccan Dialogues: Anthropology in question* (Baltimore, 1982). See also the Popular Memory Group, 'Popular memory: theory, politics, method' in Richard Johnson et al., *Making Histories* (Minneapolis, 1985).

5. In 'Writing against culture' in Richard G. Fox (ed.), *Recapturing Anthropology* (Santa Fe, NM, 1991). Lila Abu-Lughod uses 'halfie' to denote 'a person whose national or cultural identity is mixed by virtue of migration, overseas education or parentage' (p. 137). Kirin Narayan (to whom Abu-Lughod attributes the coinage 'halfie') uses 'hybridity' slightly differently to underline the way all anthropologists belong 'simultaneously to the world of engaged scholarship and the world of everyday life'; 'How native is the "native" anthropologist?', *American Anthropologist*, vol. 95, 1993, p. 681. Both terms can be extended to changes in the researcher's cultural make-up through prolonged exposure to the 'field'.

6. Deniz Kandiyoti, 'Strategies for feminist scholarship in the Middle East', paper presented to the Middle East Studies Association, November 1993; see also Irvin C. Schick on the dangers of relativism, 'Representing Middle Eastern women: feminism and colonial discourse', *Feminist Studies*, vol. 16, no. 2, Summer 1990, p. 15.

7. Chandra Mohanty, 'Under Western eyes: feminist scholarship and colonial discourses' in Mohanty, Russo and Torres (eds), *Third World Women and the Politics of Feminism* (Bloomington: University of Indiana Press, 1991, pp. 53–7); Marnia Lazreg, 'Feminism and difference: the perils of writing as a woman on women in Algeria', *Feminist Studies*, vol. 14, no. 1, Spring 1988, pp. 81–107; also *Inscriptions*, special issue on 'Feminism and the Critique of Colonial Discourse', nos 3/4, 1988.

8. Asad, 'The Concept of Cultural Translation', pp. 160–6.

9. Yet a questionnaire carried out among women in Bourj Barajneh camp in the 1970s also found a longing for change: Ghazi Khalili, *al-Mar'a al-Filastiniyya wa'l-thawra* (Beirut, 1977).

10. Partha Chatterjee, 'Colonialism, nationalism, and colonized women: the contest in India', *American Ethnologist*, vol. 16, no. 4, November, 1989: 623–5.

11. For an excellent study of Palestinian women and the resistance in Lebanon see Julie Peteet, *Gender in Crisis* (New York, 1991). Peteet also gives useful background on the history of the Palestinian women's movement.

12. An interesting exception is provided by Khadija Abu Ali who, with other GUPW members, conducted a small survey of women in the Resistance, publishing the results in book form: *Muqaddima hawl waqi' al-mar'a wa tajribatiha fi al-thawra al-Filastiniyya* (Beirut, 1975). On the GUPW, see Rosemary Sayigh, 'Palestinian Women and Politics in Lebanon' in Judith Tucker (ed.), *Arab Women: Old boundaries, new frontiers* (Bloomington: Indiana University Press, 1993).

13. The Women's Union was one of the few PLO organizations that managed to carry on after 1982. But it was seriously weakened by intra-Resistance conflict following the Fateh split of 1983.

14. It may be objected, rightly, that any research subject may be observed within the scope of familiarization, without offence to fieldwork ethics. My point is that this will not reveal structural and cultural differences within the research community as would open discussion.

15. All names used are fictional.

16. *Gender in Crisis*, p. 17.

17. Suad Joseph, 'Feminization, familism, self, and politics: research as a mughtaribi' in Soraya Altorki and Camelia El-Solh (eds), *Arab Women in the Field* (Syracuse: Syracuse University Press, 1988), pp. 39–44.

18. Lila Abu-Lughod, *Veiled Sentiments* (Berkeley: University of California Press, 1986), p. 17.

19. Dwyer, *Moroccan Dialogues*, pp. xvii, 265.

20. Eleni Varikas uses this evocative phrase in 'Gender and national identity in fin de siècle Greece' in *Gender and History*, vol. 5. no. 2, Summer 1993, p. 274; for a similar conceptualization, see Stree Sakti Shanghatana, 'Writing about women's struggles' in *'We Were Making History': Women and the Telengana Uprising* (London, 1989). See Kumkum Sangari and Sudesh Vaid who argue less for a feminist historiography than for a universal 'historiography which acknowledges that each aspect of reality is gendered': Introduction to their *Recasting Women: Essays in colonial history* (New Delhi, 1989: 2–3).

21. Marjorie Shostok, '"What the Winds Won't Take Away": The Genesis of Nisa—the Life and Words of a ! Kung Woman', in Personal Narratives Group (ed.), *Interpreting Women's Lives* (Bloomington: Indiana University Press, 1989: 231–2).

22. Vincent Crapanzano, 'Life histories: a review essay', *American Anthropologist*, 86, 1984: 956–7.

23. Dorinne Kondo puts this argument subtly and cogently in her *Crafting Selves* (Chicago: Chicago University Press, 1990).

24. Abu-Lughod, *Writing Women's Worlds*, p. 31. Ronald Grele similarly points to the danger of over-emphasizing the individual inherent in the oral history interview: *Envelopes of Sound: The art of oral history* (New York, 1991).

25. Luisa Passerini, *Italian Fascism in Popular Memory* (Cambridge, 1987); see also the Popular Memory Group, 'Popular memory', on ways that life-stories should be read.

26. Passerini, *Fascism*, p. 19.

27. Patai underlines class differences between women in Brazil in recording life-stories: only rich women refused to record (but if they agreed, they talked more): Daphne Patai, *Brazilian Women Speak* (New Brunswick, 1988), p. 4/5.

28. Patai, *Brazilian Women*, p. 8.

29. Abu-Lughod, *Writing Women's Worlds*, p. 18.

30. *Brazilian Women*, p. 8; see also Daphne Patai, 'Ethical problems of personal narratives, or, who should eat the last piece of cake?', *International Journal of Oral History*, vol. 8, no. 1, February 1987, where, again, no solution is proposed except researcher awareness.

31. Rina Benmayor, 'Testimony, action research, and empowerment: Puerto Rican women and popular education' in Sherna Gluck and Daphne Patai (eds), *Women's Words* (New York, 1991).

32. Audiences did in fact have this effect, as when a (male) visitor interrupted an older woman's story of her wedding by instructing her, 'Tell about the land you owned!'

33. Peteet quotes women telling her 'We're all liberated now because of the Resistance', suggesting that this was part of a discourse 'reserved for visitors' (*Gender in Crisis*, p. 17).

34. Sherna Gluck, 'Advocacy oral history: Palestinian women in resistance' in *Women's Words*, pp. 164–5, 206–7.

35. Marjorie Mbilinyi, '"I should have been a man": politics and labor process in producing personal narratives' in Personal Narratives Group (ed.), *Interpreting Women's Lives* (Bloomington, Indiana University Press, 1989: 219–23).

36. Abu-Lughod, *Writing Women's Worlds*, pp. 37, 41.

37. Several incidents during fieldwork demonstrated exclusionary practices against women accused of immorality: when a bomb was placed against the home of a woman whose daughter was said to be 'loose', Umm Khaled cautioned me against a sympathy visit. Later, when their home was destroyed by fighting, this family was denied a rebuilding indemnity.

Index